Essential Articles 2014

Articles, opinions, arguments, personal accounts, opposing viewpoints

In print in this book & online as part of Complete Issues

Complete Issues

articles • statistics • contacts

Essential Articles 2014
Understanding our world

Complete Issues
Fact File 2014

Complete Issues
Key Organisations 2014
Contacting our world

Complete **Issues**

articles • statistics • contacts

WITHDRAWN

Your log in details:

Username: _____

Password: _____

D0783971

Essential Articles 2014

Essential Articles 2014 is part of Complete Issues, a unique combination of resources in print and online.

Complete Issues

Complete Issues gives you the articles, statistics and contacts to understand the world we live in.

The unique format means that this information is available on the shelf and on the screen.

How does Complete Issues work?

Using www.completeissues.co.uk you can view individual pages from this book on screen, download, print, use on whiteboards and edit to suit your needs. It makes Essential Articles even more flexible and useful.

As well as being able to access all these articles in both PDF and editable formats, there are references and links to other parts of Complete Issues.

The articles in the Essential Articles series, the statistics in Fact File and the contacts in Key Organisations work beautifully together on the Complete Issues website to produce a choice of relevant writing, figures and links for further research. Teachers and librarians can instantly produce a package of well written articles, up-to-date statistics and current contacts just by entering a topic.

Complete Issues works like a mini search engine: when you enter a topic you instantly generate a listing of relevant articles, figures and organisations with a thumbnail of the page and a short description.

The **advantages of Complete Issues** over just googling are:

- **varied & reliable sources**
- **moderated - so appropriate to student use**
- **properly referenced**
- **beautifully presented**
- **adaptable for classroom use**
- **cleared for copyright**

Users can search and browse individual elements of Complete Issues or all the parts together, past and present editions.

Students can research a topic secure in the knowledge that they will find reputable sources and considered opinions.

In addition to the online service, you have this attractive printed version always available. Its bright, magazine-style format entices readers to browse and enjoy while learning about current issues and dilemmas, making even difficult issues approachable.

Because you have both the book and online access you can use Essential Articles in different ways with different groups and in different locations. It can be used simultaneously in the library, in the classroom and at home.

Your purchase of the book entitles you to use Complete Issues on one computer at a time. You can find your access codes on your covering letter or by contacting us. It is useful to record them on page 1 of this volume.

You can also buy an unlimited site licence to make the service and the material available to **all** students and staff at **all** times, even from home.

If you do not yet have the other resources in Complete Issues (Fact File and Key Organisations) you can sample the service and upgrade here:

www.completeissues.co.uk

Complete Issues

articles · statistics · contacts

Contents

“ Three young Britons showed the world just who we are. A ginger bloke from Milton Keynes, a mixed-race beauty from Sheffield, an ethnic Somali given shelter here ”

Page 36

Photo: Debenhams

Contents

" We are running away. We're going back to Texas to start a new life as far away from my father as we can get. "
Page 76

Acs. No.
WITHDRAWN
Class No.
001 ESS

66 Get some macaroni cheese and a glass of red down your throat. It won't kill you. 99
Page 98

Photo: Thomas Demol

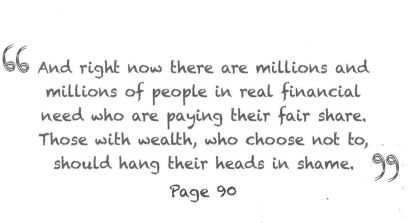

66 And right now there are millions and millions of people in real financial need who are paying their fair share. Those with wealth, who choose not to, should hang their heads in shame. 99

Page 90

Contents

> 66 I like the thought of feminist ninjas twisting the fingers of groping hands and pinching catcalling tongues. 99
> Page 104

> 66 If I had listened to the initial advice I was given, or not been able to stand up for myself, I would now be dead. 99
> Page 120

Contents

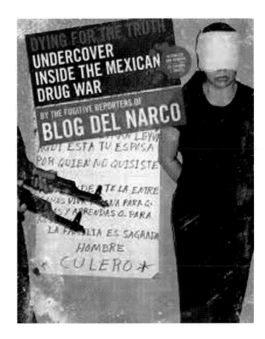

> *The idea that Britain is now what could be called a peaceful society is wishful thinking.*
> Page 150

> *We have reached a point where the main reason to have children is to make sure someone in the house knows how to work the telly.*
> Page 132

Photo: Robert Maltby

Contents

Photo: fmua/Shutterstock.com

> 66 Not all Christians are sexist, homophobic, anti-contraception, and pro-life to the point of death. 99
>
> page 160

> 66 We expect Iraq to be bombed, and so the victims remain faceless to us. 99
>
> page 174

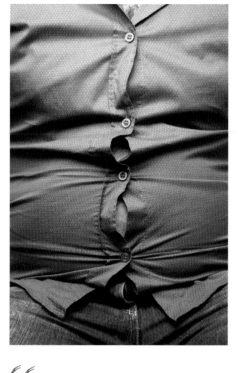

> A sixteen year-old girl told me that she had never walked out of her home alone and didn't want to
> page 204

> More and more young people do not believe a degree is worth the paper it is printed on.
> page 190

Animals

Young orangutan, by Ian Wood

"A FACE LIKE A SURPRISED COCONUT..."

SOME ISSUES:

Do you think humans needs should come before the needs of wild animals?

Who is responsible for protecting the environment of these animals?

What can be done to help these orangutans?

Selected from Complete Issues:
Rainforest risk
Fact File 2010 page 47

...that's how multi-award winning author Sir Terry Pratchett described orangutans, and it would be hard to disagree looking at these photos of energetic youngsters. Yet they and their world are endangered by the demands that we and our world make on their environment.

The last strongholds of orangutans are in Indonesia and Malaysia. Illegal logging has already devastated protected areas here, and they are now threatened by another industry.

Indonesia and Malaysia are the world's largest palm oil producers and our demand for this commodity is increasing every year. It is used in many processed foods including ice cream, chocolate, chips, cereals, frozen foods, margarine, biscuits, cakes and breads and even fruit juice. It's also in cosmetic and household products including soap, toothpaste, shampoo, cosmetics, soap powders and detergents. Increasingly it is marketed as a 'green' biofuel for vehicles. To feed this demand, the tropical rainforest is being destroyed and converted to oil palm plantations, where nothing else can grow.

Dr Fikri, Orangutan Foundation vet with rescued adult female orangutan, February 2013

Fires have also caused terrible destruction to Indonesia's forests and killed, orphaned and displaced many orangutans. A combination of factors: dry debris from logging, use of fire by palm oil companies and a longer than normal dry season have allowed fire to devastate a huge area. Some campaigning groups have suggested that the fires have been started deliberately to clear the forests.

ORANGUTANS LIVE IN THE TROPICAL RAINFORESTS OF BORNEO AND SUMATRA (PART OF INDONESIA AND MALAYSIA). THEY DEPEND ON THE FOREST TO SURVIVE

MINING HAS CAUSED IRREVERSIBLE DAMAGE - ILLEGAL OPEN CAST MINING FOR GOLD HAS TURNED THE LUSH RAINFOREST INTO A BARREN AND LIFELESS DESERT

Adult male orangutan by Ian Wood

Last tree standing with stranded orangutan

The Orangutan Foundation protects the orangutan but also recognises that their habitat is unique in its richness of biodiversity and crucial for local communities who are as dependent on the forest as is the orangutan.

Conservation, in their view, is more than protecting a species, it is about saving nature which includes us, 'the fifth ape.'

Source and photos:
The Orangutan Foundation
www.orangutan.org.uk

Neither cuddly, nor evil – why do foxes make fools of us all?

Our common sense about foxes has been eroded by the fantasies of film - it is time for some sanity to return to the debate

TERENCE BLACKER

> Forget the bulldog, the lion rampant, the unicorn or the dragon.

There is now only one animal which perfectly represents the confused state of British culture, half-fearful and half-sentimental, and that is the fox. In the wild, it is a survivor – clever, resourceful and good at adapting to the circumstances in which it finds itself. Through no fault of its own, it also brings out the worst in humans.

Foxes are in the doghouse again. In fact, they are increasingly in human houses, snacking on leftovers, cat-food and, very occasionally, babies. To those who live in the country, the behaviour of the urban foxes variety might seem odd and unnatural, like much that goes on in towns, but the recent case of four-week-old Denny Dolan, attacked in south-east London, has confirmed that they behave very differently to their rural cousins.

Another fox-panic is upon us. Mayor Boris Johnson has declared that something must be done about them; Chris Packham, the TV presenter, has rather more sensibly described that sort of reaction as "embarrassing".

No animal reveals our confused attitudes towards the natural world as clearly as the fox, and the latest incident has seen idiocy on both sides. There are those for whom foxes, like rats, represent the dangerous wild which threatens our health and the lives of babies and pets. These people believe that year by year the Demon Foxes are growing bigger and yet, paradoxically, are also starving and therefore liable to scavenge on waste, before moving into our gardens and then our houses. It is a scary Hollywood vision of a natural world evolving in a mysterious and monstrous way, which has been good box office from The Birds to Jaws. Now it is being taken seriously, even by the Mayor of London.

Ranged against them, there are those who see only the

SOME ISSUES:

Do you think foxes should be looked after, or are they too much of a threat?

Why do foxes have two very different images?

Cuddly Fox. For them, the sight of a wild animal close to humans is such a delight that the contact should be encouraged by regular food and domestication. The Cuddly Fox provides entertainment; it is like a pet which has gone interestingly feral.

Speaking for the Cuddly Fox tendency, the RSPCA has not only opposed a cull, but has suggested that people should remove undergrowth from gardens and use only fox-proof bird-feeders. In other words, the habitat and food of insects and birds should be sacrificed so that foxes are not led into temptation.

This absurdly muddled attitude is hardly surprising. It was only a few weeks ago that the RSPCA had been in full cry against the master and huntsman of the Heythrop Hunt, spending an eye-watering £326,000 on their prosecution within months of having pleaded poverty. Their default position of presenting animals as victims is in its way as silly as those who see them as source of fear and lurking danger.

Sentimentalising or demonising a species reveals how common sense has been eroded by the fantasies of film, whether produced by Disney or Spielberg. The fact is that foxes, like other animals, are neither a threat to humans nor a cosy companion. They are opportunists who will take food where they find it; they are in towns because humans, far filthier than any so-called vermin, like to leave their uneaten food on the street.

Nor have they suddenly developed a taste for human flesh, like a man-eating tiger in India. They are responding, like any animal, to changes in their environment. If foolish humans encourage them into the garden and even the house, they will see those places as a potential source of food.

It is time for a small element of sanity to return to this debate. These are wild animals. If one is sick, it should be destroyed. If a population is out of control, the local council should take action. It is stupid and inhumane to relocate them to the country.

The desire to persecute them as pests or, on the other hand, to cosset them as semi-pets is an insult not only to their wildness, but to our own intelligence.

© *The Independent, 11 February 2013*
www.independent.co.uk

> Speaking for the Cuddly Fox tendency, the RSPCA has not only opposed a cull, but has suggested that people should remove undergrowth from gardens and use only fox-proof bird-feeders. In other words, the habitat and food of insects and birds should be sacrificed so that foxes are not led into temptation.

A dog's life

Catriona Stewart: My neighbour's dog is in therapy...

She says it looks sad all the time, won't stop howling. Did I mention the dog is a Basset hound? I think the phrase "hangdog look" was designed specifically for the Basset hound.

He's a cute wee thing, right enough, though his ears just skim the ground when he walks, giving him the air of a man too tired of life to hold his head up. I always give him a special chuck under the chin, as a hint. He never takes it.

In lieu of a dog I sometimes take my godson for a walk in the park. It's quite eye-opening. There's a wee scrappy white pooch whose dolly-bird owner puts a pink bow in its hair. I asked its name once, out of politeness. Frank. He's called Frank. I wonder if he's having counselling too.

There's a dog walker, a professional, who talks to her charges like they're nursery pupils. They all sit very nicely when told to and eat their treats. There's one little dull brown terrier that never seems to sit at quite the right time and always misses out on the biscuits. It must be hard for it.

My friend Nikki lets me walk her Irish setter sometimes. Zac's a fairly unreconstructed dog. He likes mud and chasing things and he looks at you when you call him as if the word "Zac" seems slightly familiar but not very interesting.

The last time I had him out he ran over to a dog wearing a raincoat that matched its owner's Hunter wellies. He was just being personable but the lady was extremely ticked off. Her dog seemed not to be allowed houndish enthusiasm. Maybe it's me, though. Maybe I allow Zac too long a leash.

My counsellor says the reason I don't fetch the stick back is due to my deep-seated attachment issues. My owner returned to work when I was just a puppy.

SOME ISSUES:

Do you think owning a dog is a big responsibility?

Is it comparable to raising a child?

Do you think a dog might really need therapy?

Selected from Complete Issues:
Pet population
Fact File 2013 p24

I wonder what the Basset woofs to its counsellor about. I wonder about this when I'm in the park, trying to eavesdrop on the dogs' conversations.

"My counsellor says the reason I don't fetch the stick back is due to my deep-seated attachment issues. My owner returned to work when I was just a puppy." Sympathetic howls. "Mine says I chase cyclists because I was the runt of the litter and need to assert dominance over something unthreatening." Ruff.

I used to think it would be quite nice to be a dog but maybe I'm wrong. For once I'm thinking how glad I am to be human.

The Herald, 22 March 2013

Photo: Vitalijs Barisevs/Shutterstock.com

Art & culture

charging fans to download music videos is just a sign of the times

ELISA BRAY

Photo: Northfoto/Shutterstock.com

Prince unveils new track then charges fans to download the video: his rock'n'roll revolution is right on the money

Last week, Prince dared to do something unheard of. The funk star charged his fans £1.13 to download the video for his new song, "Screwdriver".

Outraged fans took to railing on Twitter: "Way to alienate your core audience Mr. Purple Badness," said one. "Tight arse – I'm sure he doesn't need the money," said another. But what difference does it make whether Prince is a million-selling recording artist or a struggling up-and-coming singer-songwriter? Every musician is entitled to be paid for their musical output – or is this something that we've forgotten in a world of YouTube and Spotify?

Bearing in mind that Prince had his fans' pockets firmly in mind when he charged an affordable £31.21 for his O2 residency shows, and then gave away two albums to fans for free, he cannot be accused of ripping off his fans. Prince has, however, consistently resisted YouTube and other unauthorised postings of his music and performances – he once blocked live footage of himself covering Radiohead's "Creep" at Coachella.

Asking fans to pay a mere £1.13 – less than the average price of a cup of coffee on the UK high street – for the privilege of downloading the video for his new song to watch any number of times, is a reasonable request.

SOME ISSUES:

Do you download music for free?

Do you think music should be free to listen to and watch?

In the age of free downloads, how are musicians expected to earn a living?

What do you think about campaigns like this one?

See also:

Should camera phones be banned from gigs? p22

Prince is forcing people to think about paying for music, making the point that it's not a commodity to be taken for granted and helping to restore the value of music.

More importantly, by charging fans for a music video when people are used to streaming content for free on YouTube, Prince is forcing people to think about paying for music, making the point that it's not a commodity to be taken for granted and helping to restore the value of music.

Similarly, when Radiohead asked fans to pay what they thought their album In Rainbows was worth in 2007, they questioned the way things are done and forced fans to consider the value of music. It was a template that posed little risk for the band since Radiohead could afford it should the experiment have backfired, so it's interesting that an up-and-coming artist has braved the same thing with his debut album, when he had so much more at risk. Brighton-based singer-songwriter Charley Bickers put out Our Frail Hearts on 28 January, streaming the album from Charleybickers.bandcamp.com and letting those who hear it name their price on the site.

Initially, Bickers was going to give the album, a collection of intricate piano-and-guitar-led songs featuring contributions from members of The Verve and Fyfe Dangerfield, away for free, but fans suggested he "did an In Rainbows" and invite contributions.

"I was going to give the whole thing away for free because I wanted to get as many people as I could to listen to my music," he explains. "Without the weight of a huge marketing campaign behind me, the only way to do it is through word of mouth."

In the fortnight since its release, he's had some interesting results. The album has been streamed 6,000 times, but with just under 300 downloads, he can see that 20 per cent choose to invest, with contributions ranging from £1 to £15.

"I thought a higher percentage would choose to contribute, but, on the whole, when they do contribute, they contribute quite generously. I found that the older generation were more willing to pay."

Still, making the album available as a pay-what-

Photo: Northfoto/Shutterstock.com

you-think-it's-worth download forces every music fan who stops by his site to consider the value of music. Bickers agrees. "One of the great things about campaigns like this is that hopefully, even if just for a split second, it forces someone to consider the value that music and the arts bring to their life." It's a step in the right direction.

© The Independent, 24 February 2013
www.independent.co.uk

"One of the great things about campaigns like this is that hopefully, even if just for a split second, it forces someone to consider the value that music and the arts bring to their life."

A.C. Grayling: What makes us human?

Culture is what separates us from the rest of the living world

According to genetics, there is not much that makes us human; depending on how you count, we share 98.5% of our genes with chimpanzees...

... Perhaps this is not such a significant matter, given that we also share about 60% of our genes with tomatoes. As this shows, human beings are fully part of nature, and the elements that make us make not just the rest of the animal and vegetable kingdoms, but the rocks beneath our feet and the stars in the sky above us.

So what does make us human? It is not that we live in social groups: ants, antelopes and sparrows do the same. It is not that we have nuanced emotional lives: so do dogs and baboons. It is not even that we have language, for other things – including trees, as it happens – have communication systems, too, and it might be that some of those systems are quite complex, as appears to be the case with dolphins, for example.

But in the human case the system of communication – language – is particularly complex and flexible, with great expressive power, and this makes possible the phenomenon of culture. If I were to pick one thing that separates humanity from the rest of the living world, culture is it.

There are two senses to the word "culture". It is used by anthropologists to talk about the traditions, practices and beliefs of a society in general. But it is also used to mean the art, literature and intellectual life of a society – and it is this that most spectacularly differentiates human beings from all other animals.

Think of history and literature, think of philosophy, politics and economics, think of schools, theatres, museums, art galleries, concert halls, libraries. Think above all of science, that wonderful achievement of the human intellect, which explores the structure and properties of the physical world, the minuscule strangeness of the quantum level, the immensities of space and time, and the intricacies of living organisms – and which then, through the application of this knowledge via technology, enables us to fly through the air; communicate around the globe at the speed of light; cure diseases; transform the world around us so that we can live in all climes at all altitudes, even in space and under the sea.

The effect of culture in this sense is not always benign: we might think of damage to the environment and the existence of weapons of war. These, too, are the results of human ingenuity. But serious as they are, the many positive aspects of what humans make and do are a cause for celebration. It is only if we read and travel – the two best sources of the best kind of education – that

SOME ISSUES:

What parts of our culture do you think most strongly separate humans from other creatures?

Why do you think we have managed to develop things such as law, art and science?

Do any other creatures show behaviour that you could classify as culture?

Both science and the arts express the inventiveness of the human mind

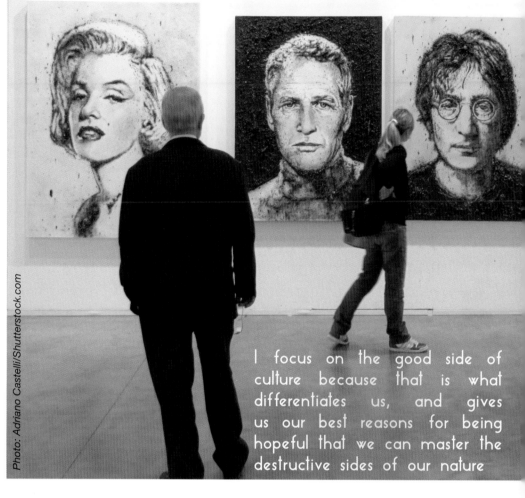

Photo: Adriano Castelli/Shutterstock.com

we see the extent of this achievement.

One part of this achievement is the development of law. Only think: if there were no laws and no institutions that administer law, life would be very insecure. The strong would prey on the weak, might would be right, we would have to be on constant guard against the depredations of others. But civilisation flourishes where laws provide protection against the excesses of a situation where "everyone has to look out for himself", for the existence of law presupposes forethought, discussion, negotiation, compromise, agreement, mutual responsibility and acceptance of the rights and interests of others. These things are the basis of community, and make it possible for most people to live together most of the time in harmony.

When we think of culture we naturally think of the arts and education along with science, and these are all the true marks of humanity at its best. Both science and the arts express the inventiveness of the human mind, but the arts capture its playfulness, too, and its desire to take the one great step that leads us even beyond knowledge: the step to understanding – understanding ourselves, our world, and our place in it.

This is the self-reflexiveness of the human mind, the ability to look at itself and to put itself into the context of everything

I focus on the good side of culture because that is what differentiates us, and gives us our best reasons for being hopeful that we can master the destructive sides of our nature

it interacts with. Chimps and dolphins can recognise themselves in mirrors, and therefore have a degree of self-reflexive awareness – but it is hard to find anywhere else in nature the sheer scale and elaboration of the human mind's response to things. The expression of that response is culture, and as the distinguishing mark of humanity, culture exemplifies what other animals lack – adaptiveness, progression, change and diversity in behaviour and activity.

I will admit that I have given an optimistic and upbeat account of human nature; cynics will wish me to remember how horrible we can be to each other, too, and

alas history provides too much support for that fact. But it is not the violent, tribal, greedy side of humanity that is distinctive; animals are territorial and can be aggressive and violent in ways wholly untempered by the occasional pangs of conscience that human beings can muster.

I focus on the good side of culture because that is what differentiates us, and gives us our best reasons for being hopeful that we can master the destructive sides of our nature, and make life and the world something that is ever closer to utopia.

New Statesman, 8 May 2013

Should camera phones be banned from gigs?

There has been plenty of brouhaha on Twitter about the evils of phones at gigs, but are they really that annoying? Bernadette McNulty is not convinced.

The latest cool war to break out in music is over the rights and wrongs of fans filming gigs on their phones and tablets. Bands and fans are up in arms about whether camera phones have become a nuisance or a boon and even whether they should be banned. Consternation has been festering for sometime but was given a good Twitter stir by musician Clint Mansell.

The former lead singer of Eighties band Pop Will Eat Itself and now feted film score composer took to the social network to vent his annoyance. About to embark on a tour, he asked his followers whether they thought that phones should be banned at gigs as they had been at some American venues, expressing his opinion that "A performance is a moment in time. Be present. Be awake. Be there. Be here. Now #rantover."

It had barely begun. As a lively discussion followed, New York trio the Yeah Yeah Yeahs posted a notice at a performance they were giving at New York's Webster Hall last week: "Please do not watch the show through a screen on your smart device/camera. Put that shit away as a courtesy to the person behind you and to Nick, Karen and Brian."

The phenomenon has definitely grown exponentially over the last three years in line with the popularity and technological advancement of smart phones. At any gig you might go to these days the searing white glow of LED lit back screens will be suspended like fairy lights over the audience: the fans are nearly as well illuminated as the stage. The arms in the air are no longer waving to the music or punching the air but are

SOME ISSUES:

Do you think camera phones are distracting when you are trying to watch a game or concert?

Do people have the right to take pictures whenever they want?

Should these things be controlled for the benefit of the audience?

See also:
Prince unveils new track then charges fans to download the video p18

Photo: Debby Wong/Shutterstock.com

Please do not watch the show through a screen on your smart device/camera. Put it away as a courtesy to the person behind you

bristles of tensed and frozen tripods. And often, as the Yeah Yeah Yeahs point out, they are in the way of the people behind you.

Except if that person is me. Because, to be honest, amongst the multitude of irritants I have to encounter if I am trying to review a concert I have barely noticed the irritation of phones being thrust in my way. As an average-sized woman (just about, although I can see that next generation pushing me into the short category) who is professionally employed to review live music, seeing the stage has been an ongoing battle for most of my life. It's not just that I am aware that

there are still on average more men at gigs, and that they are biologically taller than you, and that they will practically not notice when they are standing in front of you, blocking your view. It's that most venues are not purpose built with raked floors to suit this purpose.

They are often narrow and flat. And now, with the popularity of gig-going, packed to the rafters. The stages are often too low, or with old music hall stages, too high. I spent the whole of the one of the Pixies reunions staring at Frank Black's shoes (black, leather, clumpy). Usually, if I am lucky I will find a chink of space between someone's neck and the shoulder next to them. Sometimes, this might involve standing on tiptoe and praying that those people do not move, which of course they do, after which I must hunt for another vantage point. At the end of a night, my back in spasms, I can barely walk.

I have mentally compiled lists of good and bad venues and increasingly find myself choosing music

on whether it is being played in seated or non-seated venues. So this is why people get into classical music – not a growing aural sophistication but a longing to sit down and be able to see.

But sitting at a pop gig never quite feels right, a bit like a child sitting down in front of the TV to watch Top of the Pops. (My parents would remain seated, while watching me, with great hilarity, throw myself into ecstatic shapes.)

Photo: Debby Wong/Shutterstock.com

What I have also noticed is that I stop noticing, and the people around me stop whatever else it is they are doing, if the band is good enough.

To watch a gig is to move with it, to physically feel the music and simultaneously the people around you. That also involves noticing that other human beings can be right pains as they talk, get drunk, snog, fart, have big hair or bad body odour or sharp elbows or insist on filming the whole thing on their phone. It is only when we show awareness of each other, and respect, that this stops.

What I have also noticed is that I stop noticing, and the people around me stop whatever else it is they are doing, if the band is good enough. Nobody of course watches the terrible footage they bring home and their memory will most likely be of aching arms and other people's passive-aggressive tutting. They are in a moment, but as Mansell argues perhaps not the right one. But banning camera phones starts to push gigs on the road that jazz, classical and particularly opera went down in past centuries into the realm of rarefied and therefore exclusive experience. Audiences used to talk or even eat their way through opera in the baroque period. Now people wouldn't dare but as a result, fewer people go to see these kinds of music.

Pop is also increasingly reliant on money from the mobile-phone sponsors whose cameras the cool kids say are stealing gigs' souls. I think they should make an uneasy truce and accept the challenge of letting their music rise above the addictive glow of the video light.

Daily Telegraph, 12 April 2013
© Telegraph Media Group Limited 2013

Nobody of course watches the terrible footage they bring home and their memory will most likely be of aching arms and other people's tutting.

Body image

One size doesn't fit all

Jada

Size 18 model and face of the recent Plus Size Fashion Week

SOME ISSUES:

What does the Debenhams store group hope to gain from this?

Did they choose the right sort of models to represent a range of people?

Will this have any effect?

See also:
Model scouts outside anorexia clinics... p32

Selected from Complete Issues:
Airbrushing is out
Essential Articles 14 p32
Missing model to role model
Essential Articles 13 p42

(see also Fact File 2014 for attitudes to body image)

In April 2013 Debenhams broke with convention and displayed the clothes in its **'High Summer Look Book'** using models in a diverse variety of ages, sizes and looks.

The aim was to challenge the fashion industry by showing that a broader range of body and beauty ideals is a good thing.

Turning its back on the industry norm of young thin models, the book instead features an amputee, three models over 40 – including one nearing 70 – and a paralympian athlete. Swimwear shots celebrate curves using a model who is a size 18.

Previously the store has used size 16 mannequins to more accurately reflect the shape of customers; banned airbrushing on swimwear imagery and run lingerie campaigns featuring a 50+ model.

Stefanie Reid
Paralympian amputee makes her modelling debut

Philomena
Size 18 model, who wants to be Britain's first black plus size supermodel

Valarie
Aged 69 highlighting the fact that looking great isn't anything to do with age

The **Look Book** also features:

Tess, a size 6 petite model, who is just over 5ft tall, Lucio who is 6ft 4" tall, Maxine, aged 44 and Hugo aged 47.

Source and photos courtesy of Debenhams

Why do women let fashion gurus bring them to heel?

Colette Douglas Home

SOME ISSUES:

If high heels affect movement, are they dangerous?

Why are high heels attractive?

Why do women and not men generally wear high heels?

Is fashion sexist?

(see also Fact File 2014 for statistics on unhealthy feet)

Three women struggle across a busy road.

They totter, head forward, bottoms out. They appear drunk or sufferers of a muscular disease. One shaky, hesitant step follows another. Teeter, totter, teeter.

What is wrong with them? Nothing, except their feet are encased in the equivalent of concrete blocks. The heels of their wedge-shaped boot-shoes are six or seven inches high. So teeter, totter they go on forced tiptoe.

How ironic that the truly disabled burned up the Olympic running track on blades, while the able-bodied spend fortunes to reduce themselves to a hobble.

You might think these sky-high heels are nothing more than a lark – a bit of a laugh on a Friday night. I disagree. I see them as symbolic of something deeper: a self-inflicted injury, a betrayal even.

At the weekend the veteran French film star Catherine Deneuve called time on towering heels. She castigated women for buying into an aberration. Very high heels, she reminded us, were once the uniform of "women of ill repute" who were obliged to conform to a notion of desirability.

She said the trend for super-high heels "doesn't come from what women want. It's something that comes out of a slightly twisted desire, which makes for a rather twisted way of walking."

Its origin, she suspects – and I suspect she's right – is "in the minds of the designers who have pushed the limits – imagining an extreme woman. Everyone has fallen for it; women's magazines first and foremost."

But no-one forces women to buy them. So why, in this age of increasing equality, are women embracing them?

Deneuve says the mid-heel emancipates because it shapes itself to the arch of the foot and allows the wearer to move well, thereby adding to her allure. She's right of course. But women have form when it comes to hobbling themselves. There was a skirt of that name which held the knees in close proximity, thereby restricting movement but causing a cute wiggle.

There were, in Victorian times, corsets which gave every female an hourglass figure – but at a cost to some of curvature of the spine, rib deformity, the displacement of internal organs, breathing problems, birth defects, broken ribs and puncture wounds. What is the risk of a broken ankle by comparison?

Sheila Jeffreys, author of Beauty and Misogyny, calls very high heels "degradation with lip service to equality". If you want to see what she means take a look at the recent pictures from the Grand National meeting at Aintree. There were as many fallers in the enclosure as there were on the track.

I write this as someone who loves heels. Though I stand just shy of 5ft 10in in bare feet I have heels that range from one inch to four. But, here I agree with Manolo Blahnik, with a heel higher than four inches it is not possible to walk well – or safely.

Few if any women have a foot long enough to cope with a six or seven-inch elevation. And now Christian Louboutin says he will introduce the first eight-inch heel. I hope women leave them on the shelf.

But we look to our icons in this – for we do have a way of following the herd. For my generation

To wear heels that render the wearer effectively immobile flies in the face of everything women have achieved.

that was Princess Diana. She happened to marry a man who was a shade shorter than her so she hugged the ground in flats and we all followed.

As her marriage faltered her heels grew ever higher but they never stretched as far as those of her elder son's wife. The Duchess of Cambridge has embraced the platform, even during pregnancy.

Is she living down to Hilary Mantel's dismissal of her as a doll, a shop window mannequin? Why does she do it when she's an athlete at heart? I can't imagine.

Does it matter that so conspicuous a woman presents herself as less than she is? I fear it does. It plays into something called the Paula principle. This a phenomenon whereby women are promoted to positions two grades lower than their ability. In part the system holds them back. In part they underestimate themselves and allow themselves to be underestimated.

But aren't super-high heels only about appearance after all? Not in my opinion. If you watched the Andrew Marr show on Sunday morning you may have heard the actor Patricia Hodge talk about playing Margaret Thatcher. She said that when she had the hair-do and put on the power suits, something magical happened.

Try it for yourself with the Tony Blair pose. Sit up straight in a chair, lift your chin then place one knee at either edge of the seat and a forearm on each chair arm. Do you feel different; more powerful? If you watch the video of Mr Blair and George Bush walking together to the podium you will see they carry their arms away from their bodies. It's an alpha-male stance.

Women will say they feel empowered in heels. I can't deny it. They can transform the line of an outfit. They can add leg length

> **We revel in our own equality and freedom. Why then would we climb into the seven-inch heels just because some master cobbler has mastered the technique of making them?**

and elegance. They can lift the spirits as well as the height.

But to achieve this, they should not inhibit natural movement. To wear heels that render the wearer effectively immobile flies in the face of everything women have achieved.

There was another time and another culture which allowed foot fetishism to take hold – and it lasted until the 20th century. It happened in China and it was called foot binding.

Two decades ago I interviewed Jung Chang, the author of Wild Swans. I remember it vividly. During our discussion I held her grandmother's shoe within the palm of my hand. It was tiny. This woman (whose feet had been broken and then kept bound tight to prevent them growing) was the same age as my mother.

She had lived her life in pain. She had been unable to walk any distance, to run to feel free – and all to comply with some male fetish.

We shudder at the thought of it. We roll our eyes at the idiocy of corsets. We revel in our own equality and freedom. Why then would we climb into the seven-inch heels just because some master cobbler has mastered the technique of making them?

Back in Venice in the 1400s, when high heels first became fashionable, they sported platforms that rose to 20 inches. But the courtesans who wore them needed an entourage to support them.

It is the antithesis of the high achieving modern woman who revels in freedom, glories in her independence and hopefully remains determined to stand firmly on her own two feet.

The Herald, 16 April 2013

Just how will granny explain that tattoo in 40 years' time?

BY GAIL WALKER

We're evolving into a different species. Casting for its new drama, The Village, set in the early 20th century, the BBC had to reject the vast majority of locals who turned up to be cast as extras because ... erm ... they didn't look right.

Dyed hair, 'orange' suntans, strange piercings, plucked eyebrows and an abundance of tattoos disqualified those looking for a brief taste of stardom.

I must admit I worry about this kind of thing. What really freaks me out is all the tattoos. In the old days it was only sailors, circus strongmen and felons who made their bodies into works of dubious art.

Now it's almost compulsory – and across all walks of life. Genteel English roses turn up looking like they've got some kind of hideous skin disease creeping up their leg... until you realise it's a tat.

Presentable George Clooney types have Chinese script inked onto the side of their neck. Worse, they tell you what it means. (Actually, we all know what it means – they're gullible morons.)

Do they ever worry about when they're older and the... er... canvas becomes less taut? Sixty years from now as Grandma lies in her coffin baffled children are going to be peering intently at the wrinkly corpse, deciphering her legacy. "What does that say? Unstoppable... sex... machine. Mummy! Was granny an unstoppable sex machine?"

"No dear. She was a member of the Women's Institute."

Much of the other stuff is relatively innocuous if still disconcerting, like grey-haired men in their fifties, their skin a rich mahogany colour, their bodies pumped up on steroids. Or having coffee served by somebody with a tap washer in their ear – and through the hole in their lobe you can see customers on the other side of the cafe staring back at you, aghast.

Perhaps, we're going too far in all this identikit individualism. What's the reckoning that pretty soon looking like your own grandad is going to be the new "in".

And who knows you may even get a bit part in a period drama.

Belfast Telegraph, 3 April 2013

> *"Do they ever worry about when they get older?"*

SOME ISSUES:

What should people consider before they get a tattoo?

Does it matter what other people think about tattoos or about any other part of your appearance?

Do you agree with the writer that some 'looks' are not acceptable on older people?

Selected from Complete Issues:
Think before you ink
Essential Articles 12 p26
I hate my lizard
Essential Articles 12 p28

Model scouts outside anorexia clinics highlight fashion's own "don't ask, don't tell" policy

Rhiannon Lucy Cosslett and Holly Baxter of the Vagenda Magazine

Eating disorders are still not really regarded as diseases in the same way as cancer or malaria or measles

SOME ISSUES:

How do you think the health of models can be monitored?

Why should anorexia be taken more seriously?

Whose responsibility is it to make sure that models are eating healthily?

See also:

One size doesn't fit all p26

(see also Fact File 2014 for statistics on eating disorders)

Sarah Houston was 23 when she died after taking diet pills infused with the industrial chemical DNP, which she had bought over the internet.

The medical student had struggled with eating disorders for most of her life, crippled by the idea that she needed to lose just a little bit more weight to be passable. In absolute secrecy, she ordered the dangerous supplements which contributed to her death. Looking at the supersized pictures of this young woman gracing the tabloid news sites, you can see for yourself that she was completely beautiful; she had, to put it bluntly, model looks. But it didn't matter, because the illnesses got her. And anorexia and bulimia are illnesses. It just so happens that the way a woman dying from them looks very much the dominant western model for female beauty.

Targeting

Sarah Houston's death made the news that model scouts have been targeting patients

"We think this is repugnant. People have stood outside our clinic and tried to pick up our girls because they know they are very thin"

Photo posed by model

outside the Stockholm Centre for Eating Disorders seem, if possible, even darker. "We think this is repugnant. People have stood outside our clinic and tried to pick up our girls because they know they are very thin," a doctor at the clinic told a Swedish newspaper. One of the patients approached was so ill that she was in a wheelchair; another was just 14.

The kind of person who would do such a thing is frightening in their lack of moral compass but also completely ridiculous. You can imagine them approaching a dying, emaciated girl, whose friends and family more than anything want her to get better, to put even the tiniest morsel of food in her mouth and chew. You can see them looking into her enormous eyes as they protrude from her starved face and telling her that her legs look fabulous. Give me a call.

Glamorous

It's difficult to imagine any other disease being fetishised in a similar way – or indeed, any traumatic mental state being presented with a modicum of accuracy by the fash pack. We've seen weeping models

Shine a flattering light on the angular cheekbones. Fade out the painfully defined spine and the angry tailbone covered by a film of translucent skin

used in fashion shoots, their glamorous, silken tears glistening beautifully before the camera lens, but we've yet to see ounces of snot pouring from a runny nose pictured on the pages of Vogue.

When women suffering from anorexia, straight from the eating disorders clinic, march through the door and into the face of a waiting camera lens on the arm of a talent scout, the effect will be the same: shine a flattering light on the angular cheekbones. Fade out the painfully defined spine and the

angry tailbone covered by a film of translucent skin that renders sitting down an exercise in agony. Celebrate the tiny ankles, delicate and fawn-like in a pair of Louboutins. Hide the telltale signs of osteoporosis that lurk further up.

Airbrushing

Airbrushing a picture of anorexia into acceptability has become as second nature to some in the fashion world as perfecting the 'perfect crying face' that nobody ever manages to pull in real life. Fashion's fondness for strange, contorted positions has, after all, never manifested itself in the form of this season's coveted hernia. But what's next on this grisly conveyer belt? Perhaps cancer patients: they're skinny, after all, and could carry their excised tumours around like handbags, trailing tubes from chemotherapy drips wrapped seductively round their arms like bracelets.

Excuses

That image is crass for a reason. Anorexia and less common eating disorders are still, despite all we know and all the horror stories, not really regarded as diseases in the same way as cancer or malaria or measles. It's as though there's something silly and feminine about this decision not to eat, as though it's frivolous and even, in this world of plenty, a special sort of spoilt.

This is possibly one of the reasons why fashion continues to get away with offering tired excuses for their worship of thinness: they say the clothes look better on thin women, but as Alexandra Shulman has pointed out, that's because they're made that way. It's been argued that the very thin 'photograph better', but such an argument is obviously nonsense: we just aren't used to seeing the normal wobbles of flesh many of us carry around with us reflected in the pages of a magazine – and, as the new Debenhams look book demonstrates, when we do, it can look just as beautiful.

Take it seriously

The problem is that, even as model scouting veers on the self-parodic, even as the 'mainstream' for models becomes more narrow, even as young women die from the illness that one industry refuses to take seriously, the old adage that 'it's just boundary pushing'

always lies just around the corner.

Fashion has a special sort of get-out clause in that respect, which is why it's important to keep calling it out. Because a business model built around the idea of continually 'being outrageous' can get hideously bent out of shape in the wrong hands.

Don't ask or tell

A report on fashion scouting in Jezebel once described it as 'deliberately opaque', which seems an appropriate summary. It's the catwalk's own 'don't ask, don't tell' policy: the truth remains the same, but nobody wants to talk about it lest everybody get their Damaris knickers in a twist.

But the act of not asking or telling is downright insidious: should this model be receiving artificial nutrition on a hospital ward, rather than artfully posing with a size zero T-shirt falling off her bony shoulders? Is she underage, even prepubescent? Is she being exploited? Will this uniformity of images, those that glorify the idea of a complete bodily lack of pinchable skin and relegate the actual norm to the shameful shadows, potentially harm the people who view them? Sshh. Turn a blind eye and take the money. These sorts of issues are for doctors or politicians or sociological researchers to tackle, not the fashion experts, never mind that they all too often happen to be the perpetrators.

The time has come to lay these problems at fashion's door, because they must take their fair share of responsibility. Whoever inevitably passes the buck about what goes on outside the Stockholm Centre for Eating Disorders will demonstrate the industry's unwillingness to ever involve themselves in anything beyond

how a gypsy skirt hangs. But something has to change.

While there are myriad reasons why people develop mental illness, as well as a slew of pressures to stay slim, young and perky that don't solely emanate from fashion photography, shirking all accountability is just plain cowardly. Scouting for anorexia may be a minority activity, but it's representative of a wider malaise: one that has the potential to gnaw away at all of us every day – and one that, despite all of fashion's protestations, could easily be fixed.

New Statesman, 24 April 2013

> Should this model be receiving artificial nutrition on a hospital ward, rather than artfully posing with a size zero T-shirt falling off her bony shoulders?

Britain & its citizens

Photo:David Davies/PA Archive/Press Association Images

FACE OF THE FUTURE

Is Jessica Ennis, the face of the 2012 Olympics, also a symbol of the changes in Britain's population and attitudes?

Britain has always been a 'melting pot' society. Throughout history a constant mix of races have come to this country as migrants, as refugees, as essential workers. But we haven't always had a majority in favour of a mixed society.

In their different ways, the 2011 census and the 2012 Olympics show us that the way we think about race and identity is changing. Increasingly younger people are less concerned about racial background than their parents were.

A report from thinktank *British Future* focused on Jessica Ennis, the face of the 2012 Olympics, as someone who could also be the face of this new British identity. Their report *The melting pot generation – How Britain became more relaxed on race* suggests that 18-24 year olds (Ennis was born in 1986) are representative of a new type of Briton: "The Jessica Ennis generation can stake a strong claim to have won the race against prejudice. They are much more likely to be mixed race themselves, with one in ten children growing up with parents

Photo: Dennis Van Tine/ABACA USA/Empics Entertainment

**Zayn Malik – of boyband
One Direction, born in 1993
reflects a new British identity**

from different backgrounds; ever more likely to form mixed race relationships themselves; and much less likely to think there is any big deal about that anyway."

This contrasts strongly to earlier attitudes. In the 1950s inter-racial relationships were rare and mixed race couples often met with hostility. Ennis's parents – Vinnie who is black and from Jamaica and Alison who is white and from Derbyshire – were still breaking accepted social norms when they began a relationship in the 1980s. At that time 50% of the public were opposed to marriage across ethnic groups. A survey for the 'melting pot' report found this proportion had fallen to 12% by 2012. Public attitudes are so different now that 59% of people say they wouldn't even notice, much less react to, a mixed race couple in the street.

The twenty- and thirty-somethings who are forming relationships now are far less likely to see race as any sort of barrier to their relationship. Interestingly, Britain is even more of a melting pot than America.

In the United States the trend has been for those with any black heritage (mixed or otherwise) to define themselves as black and to marry back into the black community, as President Barack Obama did, for example. Only 10% of African Americans are in mixed marriages compared to over 40% of British born Black Caribbeans.

Race can still be an issue and a problem for those who are not obviously part of the majority. But, as a testament to changing attitudes, this extract from *The Sun* quoted in *The melting pot generation* is significant: "It was 46 golden Olympic minutes when three young Britons showed the watching world just who we are. A ginger bloke from Milton Keynes a mixed-race beauty from Sheffield, an ethnic Somali given shelter on these shores from his war-ravaged homeland. This is what Britain looks like today... the sight of these three Olympians wrapped in the Union Flag will surely do more to inspire than any political words."

The athletes mentioned were Greg Rutherford, long jump, Jessica Ennis, heptathlon and Mo Farah, 10,000 metres. When Farah was asked if he would have been still prouder to have won for Somalia he replied, "Not at all, mate! This is my country."

Concluding his contribution to *The melting pot generation,* Sunder Katwala says:

"Jessica Ennis... tells an important census story of our changing society too. Jessica Ennis is what integration looks like."

**Ennis's parents were still breaking accepted social norms
when they began a relationship in the 1980s.**

Photo: Lynne Cameron/PA Wire/Press Association Images

Jessica Ennis and her father at her wedding, May 2013

THE JESSICA ENNIS GENERATION CAN STAKE A STRONG CLAIM TO HAVE WON THE RACE AGAINST PREJUDICE

THEY ARE MUCH MORE LIKELY TO BE MIXED RACE THEMSELVES

EVER MORE LIKELY TO FORM MIXED RACE RELATIONSHIPS

AND MUCH LESS LIKELY TO THINK THERE IS ANY BIG DEAL ABOUT THAT ANYWAY

There are many people born in the 80s and 90s who reflect this new generation of mixed race Britons such as:

LEWIS HAMILTON – racing driver and 2008 Formula One World Champion, was born in 1985. His father is British Grenadian and his mother white English.

LEONA LEWIS – singer who won The X Factor in 2006, was born in 1985. Her father is of Afro-Guyanese descent, and her mother is of Welsh, Irish, and Italian descent. She has revealed how her striking mixed-race looks made her a target for bullying classmates at school.

THEO WALCOTT – footballer was born in 1989 to a black Jamaican father and a white English mother. He has said, "I'm part of a generation that doesn't think as much about race."

EMELI SANDÉ – singer who performed at both the opening and closing ceremonies of London 2012, was born in 1987. Her father is Zambian and her mother is white English. She found it difficult growing up in the only mixed-race family in a small village in Aberdeen. "As an inter-racial couple [her mum and dad] had it hard. They had to really battle just to be together back then, so I just thought I wasn't going to complain. I kind of got on with it because I knew it could have been a lot worse."

HEATHER WATSON – currently the British Number 1 women's tennis player was born in 1992 to a Papua New Guinean mother and a Manchester-born English father.

ZAYN MALIK – member of boyband One Direction, was born in 1993 to a British Pakistani father, and an English mother. Malik claims he didn't fit in at his first two schools due to his mixed heritage, but after moving schools at the age of twelve, he started taking pride in his appearance. He has quit Twitter as a result of racist abuse.

Sources: The melting pot generation –
How Britain became more relaxed on race,
British Future & others
www.britishfuture.org

Housing crisis: did damp and crowding contribute to cot death?

Kia Stone's daughter was found dead in her cot below fungus growing out of the wall in a flat on York's Chapelfields housing estate

Maggie O'Kane & Ben Ferguson

The first thing Kia Stone did when she got back to the flat was dismantle the cot in which her 11-month-old baby daughter Telan had been found dead the week before.

Above the cot in the crowded bedroom where Kia, her partner Simon and their two children had slept, a large mushroom continues to grow out of the damp plaster. The wallpaper is a violent shade of bright green, edged with black lines of damp. Wet with condensation, it hangs limply from the wall.

Kia, 24, does not know how Telan died. Neither do the doctors. Kia wonders if the damp in her single-bedroom flat on the Chapelfields housing estate in York was a contributory factor in the death of her baby girl. The autopsy report found no cause of death. But experts say that damp and overcrowding is a risk factor in cot death.

Just days after Telan's death, on 6 October, three health officials – a doctor, a health visitor and a paediatric nurse – wrote to York council warning of the increased risk of cot death to another child, Isla Jackson, who was born prematurely and spent six weeks in a special baby care unit, and was then living with a family of five in a damp, two-bedroom flat.

The letter from the health visitor Russell Dowson reads: "This property is not suitable and specifically puts Isla at an increased risk of suffering cot death."

Film-maker Peter Gordon had, by chance, been filming with the Stone family for a series of films for the Guardian's Breadline Britain series looking at poverty in Britain. Gordon's

SOME ISSUES:

If there is a shortage of housing, what can the council do to help families like this?

Could the death of Telan have been avoided?

If so how?

What can the rest of society do to assist families like this?

Selected from Complete Issues:
Supply and demand
Fact File 2011 p110

The Stones have lived in their one-bedroomed council flat for two years. It was originally intended to be temporary

film starts with a laughing Telan being gently bounced on the bed by her mother. Telan died 10 days after filming finished.

The Guardian showed the film to Prof Richard Jenkins, one of Britain's foremost experts on cot deaths. He said: "It's not clear that the fungus growing over the baby's cot is necessarily a toxic form of black mould, but it is likely to give rise to airborne spores which, when inhaled, could exacerbate a respiratory condition.

Photo: The Press, York

"Damp conditions also encourage mould and house mites and researchers have reported an increased frequency of immune response to dust mites and of minor ailments in cot death victims."

The Stones have lived in their one-bedroomed council flat for two years. It was originally intended to be temporary accommodation.

The family ran into trouble two years ago when Simon's epilepsy meant he had to give up his job as a chef at a fish and chip restaurant at the Novotel hotel in York. The family couldn't keep up rental payments on the two-bedroomed house they were living in at the time and when the owner put it on the market for £113,000 they had to move out.

"I really wanted to work. Buying that house was way out of our league. But it was perfect. I would have stayed there for the rest of my life, just built a little extension on to it, but we couldn't keep it," says Kia.

The flat they moved into on a temporary basis was then permanently assigned to them by the council. "There is a big shortage in York and they told us we had to make the flat we were in permanent or we would lose it. I can't count the number of times I phoned the council about the damp. They came and washed the black mould off – it just came back," says Kia.

By the time of Telan's death they had switched off the heating in the flat in a bid to control the damp.

"The bedroom is freezing cold but the council advised me to keep the heating

"The bedroom is freezing cold but the council advised me to keep the heating off because if it gets too warm the fungus grows"

off because if it gets too warm the fungus grows," she says.

Steve Waddington, York council's assistant director of housing and community safety, said: "Our heartfelt sympathies go to the family for their tragic loss. At this very sad time and alongside other professionals we are supporting the family while they wait for a home that better suits their needs.

"We can confirm their complaint about damp was received and that council technicians visited the house to fit new fans and to advise the family on how to help reduce condensation."

In York, the number of people waiting for council housing has increased by 70% in the last year. Nationally, the number of people waiting for council accommodation is close to 2 million, and when the government caps housing benefit payments to private landlords next April, the housing charity Shelter expects that number to soar.

York council said the growth in demand was due to the high cost of property in the city, making accommodation within the housing benefit cap hard to come by. Shelter says the average private rent in the city for a two-bedroom home is around £650 a month. For the Stones, who have a joint income of £640 a month, there are few choices about where they can live. The Labour-run council said more than 4,500 people were now on its waiting list for homes but supply was limited.

Tracey Simpson-Laing, the council's cabinet member for health, housing and adult social services, said she expected the problem to worsen. "Legislation coming into force in April 2013 could impact negatively on people living in overcrowded conditions as households eligible for housing benefit in registered social housing will be expected to contribute more to their rent if their number of bedrooms exceeds new Department for Work and Pensions guidelines."

Shelter is warning that a combination of rising rents, the shortage of suitable rental properties and the forthcoming housing benefit cap is forcing people to choose to live in overcrowded and damp conditions all over Britain. Roger Harding, head of policy, research and public affairs, said: "As changes to housing benefit start to

On 7 November, a month after her daughter's death, York council rehoused Kia Stone and her family in a two-bedroom flat.

hit, many people will try to stay put until they hit breaking point, potentially taking other measures such as overcrowding or living in poor conditions to avoid disruptive, expensive moves. Overcrowding is one of the hidden symptoms of our housing crisis. Behind closed doors, hundreds of thousands of children are suffering in cramped conditions that are doing lasting damage to their education and wellbeing." In a recent study, Shelter found that poor housing conditions increase the risk of severe ill health or disability by 25% during childhood.

The environmental health consultant Steph Harrison, a member of the Chartered Institute of Environmental Health, told the Guardian: "In 30 years working as an environmental health officer I've never seen so many cases of overcrowding as I am seeing now. It's becoming a big problem that councils must take more seriously.

"Mould grows in overcrowded houses because of the amount of laundry and cooking that goes on to feed more people in a small space. Insulation and ventilation can't cope with the extra demand."

Back in Chapelfields, Kia is on the phone to the council again. A social worker is in the front room offering counselling to the grandparents. "I can't bear it," Kia is telling York housing department. "I can't stay in this flat. I can't stand the damp and the wet."

On 7 November, a month after her daughter's death, York council rehoused Kia Stone and her family in a two-bedroom flat.

The Guardian, 19 November 2012
© Guardian News & Media 2012

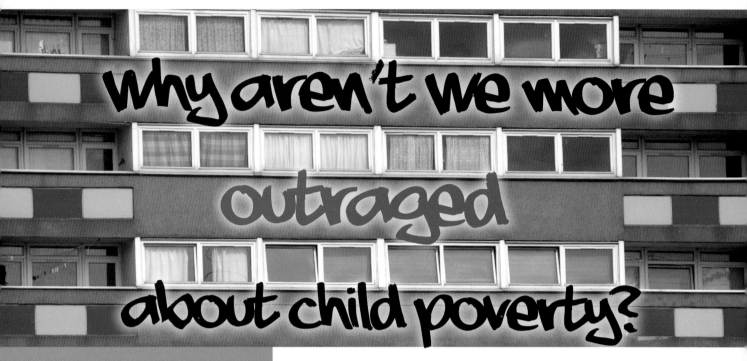

Why aren't we more outraged about child poverty?

When you talk about child poverty, you're essentially talking about fairness.

ALAN WHITE

In a hall in East London, the Reverend Giles Fraser, formerly of St Paul's Cathedral and now of St Mary's, Newington, has a question for a small group of local teenagers, all aged around 15 or 16.

"Fifty–two per cent of children in this borough live in poverty. What do you think is the average salary of people who work here?" he asks.

The guesses range from £10,000 to £18,000.

"All wrong," he replies. "It's £58,000. Because of Canary Wharf."

Fraser's been asked by the local council to find out what local children think is fair and unfair about the borough. We don't tend to hear the voices of normal kids from the rough parts of town in the mainstream media – we tend only to hear from the extremes (the famous, or the ones being glowered at by Ross Kemp because they're part of a Growing Gang Problem). It's a shame really, because the things they have to say are pretty interesting.

After spending a few hours with them, I made a list of some of the things they find unfair:

– They think that when they put their address on their CV, it makes potential employers less likely to consider them, and that's not fair. They don't like the fact that their area is known as a place where there were riots. They don't like the fact that when they go to places like Canary Wharf it's opulent and gleaming; the polar opposite of the scruffy houses near Brick Lane where they live.

– They don't think it's fair that old people in Tower Hamlets have to live in bad housing association accommodation. They'd like to volunteer to help them, but they don't know how.

– They don't think it's fair that other kids in London boroughs have more facilities, parks and open spaces. They think it's because those boroughs have better local government.

– They don't think it's fair that people who work for the council; bus drivers and the like, are constantly rude to them.

One boy: "These people are supposed to be public servants but the problem is they don't see us as members of the public."

– They don't think it's fair that their streets are scary. They'd like there to be more monitoring of places like bus stations, because gangs and drug addicts worry them.

– They don't think it's fair that they themselves often stereotype other young people – e.g. there's a tendency to think someone's a "chav" just because he's wearing a hoodie. One white kid, with a really thick East End accent, says: "Young people often think things like all Asian kids act the same: it's bang out of order, and that's mostly because of things put forward by adults in the media," at which point most of the kids – the majority of them Asian – look at me accusingly, and I take a sudden interest in my shoes.

The thing that got me about this list – and there were a load of other issues – was that I honestly don't think I'd have said any of them when I was their age. I had a middle-middle class upbringing in a largely lower-middle class town, and was accordingly insulated from the twin concepts of what was fair and what wasn't.

I wasn't scared of going out on the streets, I didn't feel like public servants were in any way opposed to me, I didn't think my postcode would have any impact on a job application, and so on. I just didn't feel like I had it much better or worse than anyone else. A bit later, with the benefit of hindsight, I realised I did. But the point is, I don't think it's fair that none of these things should have impacted on me growing up, while these kids should be worrying about all of them at once. Because frankly, childhood's tough enough.

The kids in East London spoke a lot to me about relative poverty – about children in their borough living in cheap clothes, never being able to go on holidays, not eating properly – and as their testimonies revealed, the knock-on effects of this are pernicious.

They don't think it's fair that people who work for the council; bus drivers and the like, are constantly rude to them.

They don't think it's fair that their streets are scary.

They don't think it's fair that old people in Tower Hamlets live in bad housing. They'd like to help them but they don't know how.

And the one thing that really came out of the discussions I had is exactly how unfair – and how self-perpetuating – poverty is. What the kids were saying is backed up by statistics: by 16, children receiving free school meals achieve 1.7 grades lower at GCSE than their wealthier peers. Leaving school with fewer qualifications translates into lower earnings over the course of a working life.

Basically, when you're talking about child poverty, you're talking about fairness. It's something about which we should be absolutely outraged – but we just aren't

New Statesman, 14 February 2013

"52% of children in this borough live in poverty. What do you think is the AVERAGE SALARY of people who work here?" he asks.

The guesses range from £10,000 to £18,000.

"All wrong," he replies. "It's £58,000. Because of Canary Wharf."

MUM, DAD AND THOSE DRUNKEN DAUGHTERS

Vicky Allan

ASKED to select an image that illustrates the problem of Christmas binge-drinking, many people would plump for a familiar media favourite: mini-skirted girls collapsed on street kerbs with their legs skewed out.

Young people on the lash are not, however, the focus of the latest pre-festive season alcohol awareness drive. Launched last week by the Violence Reduction Unit (VRU), the campaign opened with the testimony of Catherine Park, a mother who faced up to her own alcohol problem after waking with a hangover at 2pm on Christmas Day, having failed to get up for present-opening with her children. The look on her daughters' faces, she says, made her decide to deal with her drinking.

It is a timely reminder, since grown-up, mature drinking is a serious problem. The home, not the pub or the club, is where our national drink problem begins. That's where the cirrhosis starts.

The volume of alcohol drunk per capita has risen by 60% since 1960, and by 21% since my own childhood in 1980. Clearly, then, it's not the young of today that represent the big shift, but us adults, parents, the ones who come home and sigh, "I could do with a drink", then spend the evening knocking back a bottle of Rioja. Contrast this with my own mum and dad, who barely had a drink outside Christmas and birthdays.

Booze, of course, is just one substance of many that we are highly prone to abusing; sugar and caffeine being another two. But alcohol is unique in the way its effects extend beyond health. We can't discuss it without also talking about underage sex, teenage pregnancy, sexually transmitted diseases, street violence, domestic violence and child neglect. Alcohol misuse is estimated to cost Scotland £2.25 billion per year in extra services across the NHS, police, courts, social services and lost economic productivity.

Peer-pressure drinking among the young; the kind seen in all those late-night photos, and indulged in, we are told, by increasing numbers of girls; carries the risk of alcohol poisoning, unsafe sex and casual violence. This is the kind of drinking that provokes a lot of head-shaking and ogling, since predominantly it is about sex.

The lifetime relationship one develops with alcohol, however, is influenced not just by your peers, but by what goes on in your family.

It is partly about the predispositions you inherit, but also about what you see in the home and absorb as being the norm, which explains why the new VRU campaign is aiming to get adults, and particularly parents, thinking about their own attitudes to drinking at Christmas.

A recently published Demos report showed that a mother's drinking has a far greater impact than a father's on how much their children will drink when older. This study found that at the age of 16, teenagers were mainly influenced by their peers in how much they drank, but that by 34, the likelihood of them

SOME ISSUES:

Why do you think that there is a difference in the way the media portrays women and men with regards to drinking?

Do you think this is fair?

How do parents' drinking habits affect their children?

How much alcohol is too much?

Selected from Complete Issues:
I like a drink, but collectively we have a problem
Essential Articles 14 p11

See also:
Complete Issues
Alcohol

binge-drinking rose in line with how much they had thought, as a child, that their mother drank.

This is dispiriting news for us ladies, particularly since it seems that currently we are witnessing a backlash against female drinking. There are probably two reasons for this. Women are clearly drinking more; they have joined the men in this habit; and therefore experiencing more of the health consequences that were previously the domain of men. In the past 20 years, for instance, the number of women aged 25-29 being treated for chronic liver disease has risen seven-fold.

But the other reason is that there is still some residual idea that drunkenness is more shameful for women and that they should get back to their traditional feminine habits of abstinence. The words "shame" and "stigma" are all too often used as possible sticks to beat girls back into resisting the demon drink. This is partly because alcohol might lead to sex, but also because women are still viewed as (and often are) the main carers, the ones who bear the ultimate responsibility for children.

Some would like to see us go back to fully stigmatising women. Writing in this newspaper last year, psychologist Dr Aric Sigman suggested that "perhaps it's time Scotland re-stigmatised alcohol abuse as something shameful", adding that, since young women are most at risk from heavy drinking, "this sentiment would be all the more effective if the stigma came with a generous serving of sexual inequality: heavy drinking and drunkenness being even more 'shameful' for females".

PERSONALLY, I DON'T THINK WE CAN EVER ATTAIN SOCIAL EQUALITY WITHOUT AN EQUAL RIGHT TO GET DRUNK

GROWN-UP, MATURE DRINKING IS A SERIOUS PROBLEM

Personally, I don't think we can ever attain social equality without an equal right to get drunk. I'm inclined to agree with a friend who argues that one of the great things about the "northern drinking cultures", as opposed to the more restrained Mediterranean ones, is that they embrace the idea of men and women getting drunk together; and that this makes for a culture that treats women more equally.

So, to tackle this problem we need to talk about men as well as women. And we need to allow ourselves to treat alcohol as more than just a laugh. In Scotland, it is almost impossible to tell someone that they have a drink problem, because they will immediately point to all their friends who drink at least as much as them.

Of course, there are great things about getting drunk. There is a need, among other things, collectively to let go, to allow oneself to look a fool, and that's why many of us don't want to let go of our drinking culture. But there are consequences to this. Rather than just pretending they don't exist and knocking back another double, it is time we acknowledged that there is a balance to be found. And joking with our kids about our latest hangover might not be appropriate; even at Christmas.

Herald Scotland, 2 December 2012

Photo: veroxdale/Shutterstock.com

EDL have right to protest but ARE NOT WELCOME HERE

SOME ISSUES:

Do you think everyone should have the right to protest?

Does everyone have the right to freedom of speech?

Should there be exceptions?

Do you agree with the letter written here?

Do you think it is ever acceptable for freedom of speech to be taken away?

What side-effects might this have?

Selected from Complete Issues:
Should BNP teachers be banned?
Essential Articles 13 p61

Political and religious leaders of Manchester united to co-sign a letter about the EDL march, that took place in Manchester city centre

THE ENGLISH DEFENCE LEAGUE (EDL) is a far-right street protest movement which opposes what it considers to be a spread of Islamism, Sharia law and Islamic extremism in the United Kingdom. At many of their demonstrations, EDL members have clashed with counter-demonstrators.

THE RIGHT TO PEACEFUL PROTEST LIES AT THE HEART OF DEMOCRACY. It gives those who feel disenfranchised a voice and can make those in power listen. But one of the side-effects is that sometimes we have to put up with people we disagree with.

The EDL has decided to come to Manchester this weekend. The law protects the right of anyone to come to Manchester and the law protects the right of anyone to protest peacefully.

THEY CAN COME – BUT THEY AREN'T WELCOME. Greater Manchester is a place that is proud of its diversity, proud of its inclusion and – most of all – proud of its welcoming spirit. Manchester is renowned across the world as a place where people are made to feel at home wherever they come from. It goes to the very heart of what it means to be a good Mancunian and for that matter, a good Briton.

But we can't welcome people who spew hatred and racism. That's the EDL's message, distinctly un-English and certainly un-Mancunian. It is in stark contrast to the vision of hope and acceptance that runs through Manchester's DNA. Despite abhorring their views, our great tradition of protest, free speech and democracy means we do have to tolerate their presence, even though it is distasteful.

So how do we respond to the EDL? What is a good Mancunian response? We strongly believe that the best thing to do is to simply ignore them.

Come into Manchester as usual on Saturday: go to the cinema, go shopping, go for a meal, go for a drink and just don't acknowledge the small band of people who have nothing to do with this city or what it stands for. Turn your back as they have their moment of noise and be assured that they will go back where they came from soon enough.

Our police and city council are well versed in dealing with these matters and have a clear plan in place to minimise disruption to the city. They can be trusted to protect us. They have also made clear they will not tolerate any violence and action will be taken against anyone who breaks the law.

Events such as these are highly emotive and sensitive and polarise views of individuals. It is important that those seeking to counter-demonstrate do so lawfully, responsibly and in the spirit of the ideals they come in the name of.

BUT THE LAST THING THE EDL WANTS IS TO BE IGNORED. THE CLEAREST SIGNAL WE CAN SEND IS TO DO JUST THAT.

Manchester Evening News, 1 March 2013

WHO SIGNED THE LETTER?

Tony Lloyd (Police and Crime Commissioner)

The Right Reverend Terence Brain (Bishop of Salford)

The Right Reverend Mark Davies (Bishop of Middleton)

Raja Kaushal (Trustee, Gita Bhavan Hindu Temple)

Imam Ahmad Nisar Beg Qadri (Secretary General, Mosques and Imams National Advisory Board)

Frank Baigel (President of the Jewish Representative Council of Greater Manchester and Region)

Bishop Doyé Agama (Apostolic Pastoral Association)

Rev Andrea Jones (Area Dean, Manchester)

Lucy Powell MP (Manchester Central constituency)

Sir Richard Leese (Leader, Manchester City Council)

Councillor Simon Wheale (Leader of Liberal Democrat Group and Opposition, Manchester City Council)

Councillor Pat Karney (City centre spokesperson, Manchester City Council)

Councillor Afzal Khan CBE (Chair, Manchester Council of Mosques)

Councillor Jim Battle (Deputy Leader, Manchester City Council)

Councillor Sue Murphy (Deputy Leader, Manchester City Council)

Councillor Bernard Priest (Executive Member for Neighbourhood Services, Manchester City Council)

Vaughan Allen (Chief Executive, Cityco)

Photo: veroxdale/Shutterstock.com

It's a difficult question for any disabled person to answer: would I want to be cured?

The back-and-forth between parents on whether they'd want their child cured of Down's Syndrome made me reflect on my own condition

SARAH ISMAIL

US researchers have made a breakthrough in the search for a cure for Down's Syndrome. This week Dominic Lawson, whose daughter has the disability, argued that he would not want her cured. His daughter, he said, is who she is - the person her parents and sister know and love. A cure, he added, would give her the ability to count or read a clock, but those abilities don't matter to her family.

A parent of a five-year-old girl with Rett Syndrome, Catriona Moore, today responded to Dominic Lawson's column. She said that while she loves her daughter the way she is "unquestionably" she also wants her to be cured "more than anything in the world."

I can understand both views. I've been physically disabled since birth as a result of Cerebral Palsy, a condition for which there is, so far, no cure. There are, however, several treatments that lead to significant improvement.

But so far, I have never read a piece by a disabled person about whether they would want to be cured completely. So, would I?

Honestly, the answer is that this is a very difficult question. I am proud to be disabled, because I've never known any different. I'm proud of my parents and proud to be their child because they have accepted me, while doing everything possible to give me treatment.

My disability has allowed me to meet many people I love, who I think I would not have met if I was not disabled. I like to think my disability has made me more sensitive to all differences. It could well be the reason I don't like racism, religious discrimination or homophobia.

SOME ISSUES:

If you have, or if you developed a disability, and there was a cure for it, would you want it?

Can you understand why parents might not want to cure their child of a disability?

Selected from Complete Issues:
Choosing to sit tight
Essential Articles 15 p28

Photo posed by model

I like to think my disability has made me more sensitive to all differences. It could well be the reason I don't like racism, religious discrimination or homophobia.

I understand that these differences can't be helped. Would I understand this if I was not 'different' myself? Maybe not.

On the other hand, is there anything I would change about my disability? The honest answer is yes, there is. I would give anything to be able to drive a car – something my disability makes impossible.

My disability has also been the reason I have seen death from a young age, of people who were far too young to die. People I grew up with. People I consider my closest friends. They were more severely affected by our disability than I am. Do I wish they had been able to walk? Of course. Do I wish they had been able to talk to me? Every single day.

What would I do if I was cured? I'd buy a pair of high heels, take a driving test, pass it and drive a fast car. Then I would cure those of my friends who are still alive today and have long, clear, verbal conversations with them on long walks around a lovely park.

That's just a dream for me, though. Am I sad that it will never come true? Not really. If I put on high heels, I'd probably fall flat on my face, with or without a 'normal' ability to balance. If I drove a fast car, I'd probably crash it, with or without a disability. As for my friends, if we were all cured, I wonder if they would even want to know me. Since I would hate it if they didn't, I'll take my life exactly as it is, thank you very much.

© The Independent, 23 November 2012
www.independent.co.uk

My disability has also been the reason I have seen death from a young age, of people who were far too young to die. People I grew up with. People I consider my closest friends.

DISABILITY FOR BEGINNERS

Just over a year ago, broadcaster and journalist Mark Holdstock was diagnosed with multiple sclerosis.

Until then, he'd been **living his dream** as a presenter on BBC Radio 4.

Now he faces an all too certain future with apprehension, but also a degree of conviction.

As is so often the case with unexpected disability, the change is rapid and the learning curve is steep. I have primary progressive multiple sclerosis. I first knew something was wrong when I was dropped from the early morning food and rural affairs radio programme I presented, Farming Today. I was doing too many retakes during the recording. To be fair, neither the management nor I realised that I was showing the early signs of a degenerative illness, where the body's immune system attacks its own nervous system.

Confirmation came in an MRI scan, showing the telltale signs of white scarring, scars which give the name to the sclerosis part of the condition. I was embarking on a journey, an unwanted, and unexpected journey, where my body and speech would start behaving badly.

My life was changing and I had to learn to adapt. Ahead were a variety of delights, a kind of pick-and-mix. Select from double incontinence (fortunately yet to appear), eyesight disturbance (also yet to strike) and mobility problems ... appearing fast. Combine that with the impact on my speech, which effectively ended my radio career, and I am having to adjust to change.

It's a learning process, and as a lifelong broadcaster, journalist and writer, the most obvious thing was to write about what is happening in a blog.

SOME ISSUES:

Do you think writing a blog is a good way of dealing with changes in your life? Why?

Do you think a person has the right to refer to themselves however they like, even if other people find it offensive?

Selected from Complete Issues:
More than words
Essential Articles 13 p137

I take a straightforward view. I would never call somebody else a cripple, unless they asked specifically to be described as such, but I absolutely reserve the right to describe myself as I wish

I knew I was in effect training for a new life. I called the blog The Trainee Cripple.

The sound of tutting was pretty swift. Some people objected ... the word does upset some people as being derogatory. I take a straightforward view. I would never call somebody else a cripple, unless they asked specifically to be described as such, but I absolutely reserve the right to describe myself as I wish, and the naming of this blog, which is about me, and the impact of MS on my life, is my decision.

Of course, I wouldn't be the first to upset others by reclaiming a term which has previously been used as a term of abuse. The gay community reappropriated the word queer in the 1990s as a strident reaction to the attitudes of politicians towards homosexuals during the years of Margaret Thatcher's Conservative government. It's become a tool of empowerment, and at a time when disabled people are under attack from those in power, the use of the word cripple by myself, about me, perhaps reduces the power of the weapons that they are using against us. Maybe it makes those who are being abusive face reality.

What I don't know yet, and I haven't made my mind up about, is the degree to which I want to become part of a community, and with it an activist. I have always been politically aware, it comes with the territory of the work which I did. One of the differences now is that no longer being a BBC name, I can now shout about it, and use what skills I picked up as a broadcaster and journalist to make those views heard.

The question is whether I have the energy to, that is part of my training as a cripple, become an active part of the community that I'm reluctantly joining. In a way, writing

about it is as much for me as for others, pointing out some of the things like seats in shops or in concert hall bars. Things which have never occurred to me in the past.

Am I joining a community, am I going to be participating? Perhaps, one of the consequences of MS is fatigue and that will be a factor. Writing is something I can do within the envelope of that fatigue.

I am beginning to learn where there are limits, I'm beginning to learn where there might be discrimination, sometimes unintended. The use of the word cripple about myself is, I admit, provocative ... but it's meant to be.

You can read more about Mark on his blog:
http://traineecripple.blogspot.co.uk

Disability Now, March 2013

I'm on benefits but I'm no scrounger

Writing on the Money Saving Expert website, Ross Goodall from Southampton responds to the headlines depicting those in receipt of Disability Living Allowance as scroungers.

I have had enough. I am not a scrounger, and this is why.

I am in the unenviable position of claiming disability living allowance and incapacity benefit because I have developed a giant cell tumour of bone in my right wrist.

The tumour is very rare, but it's now the size of a cricket ball. This means my hand is no longer attached to my wrist.

The pain is intense and constant. I cannot pick up my children the way most fathers can. I cannot play catch with my son, or even hold a cup of coffee in my right hand. All of these things people take for granted, and there must be thousands of people worse off than me.

I have worked all my life, as a mechanical engineer, IT specialist and even a bus driver. When I found myself in the position where, for the first time in my life I had to claim, I was and am disgusted at how 90% of people treat you as a benefit claimant.

Try going for a job interview with my arm

When I go for job interviews, and I have to explain why I cannot shake the interviewer's hand on entry, or I take my coat off and they see my arm, the interview is over.

I get one of two reactions without fail: "How much disruption is the treatment going to cause if you get the job?" Or: "That's an insurance liability."

No matter what you are claiming or why, you are deemed and treated as a scrounging fraud until you prove otherwise. One is treated as guilty until proven innocent.

I am not just talking about the Department for Work and Pensions, but also the people I meet everywhere I go, every day.

The look of disgust and judgement as you hand over a state Healthy Start voucher for milk and veg at the supermarket. Or when you meet someone new and receive "and what do you do for a living?" and you watch the expression on their face when you say you are not working.

Oh sure, everyone is fine once they have seen the size of my wrist and how it has deformed my hand.

Ridiculous myth

Since the debate on capping benefits at £26,000 a year, people seem to think all benefits recipients get that. I wish. I have two young children and a partner to support on a smidgen over £11,000 a year.

SOME ISSUES:

Why do you think people on benefits get so much press attention?

What does this person's account make you think of people on benefits?

Selected from Complete Issues:
The demonisation of the disabled is a chilling sign of our times
Essential Articles 15 p23

Ross Goodall's own picture of the tumour on his arm

With the increase in utility costs over the past year, hand-in-hand with a drop in my entitlement, there is a simple choice to make. Treat the children without watching the purse strings, or keep the boiler running and the lights on.

On average, gas and electric costs £30-£40 a week depending on the season. We are on a prepayment meter to clear the debt we accrued when I was forced out of work by my tumour. Therefore, we cannot move supplier, it's that simple.

Is the taxpayer paying off my credit cards and loans? No. I don't have a bank account, credit card or loan.

Do we have any other luxuries? Yes, we have a flat panel TV, bought for us by my mum a few years ago. Do we have any games consoles? Yes, bought by a friend who has helped us so much, we have no idea what we would have done.

What little we have is bought and paid for – normally not by us, as once we have fed ourselves and paid the bills there is never anything left.

There are no pints down the pub either. In fact, I haven't been inside a pub in four years. I don't miss it, but it is something else most take for granted that we never get to do.

Our budget is so tight that if an emergency crops up, like me being rushed to hospital because the delirium from the pain has caused me to pass out and collapse down the stairs – which happened just before Christmas – there is no way to get me home from hospital.

When we go food shopping, it is worked out to the absolute penny. There can be no deviation as there is nothing to play with.

Yes, we have a 17-year-old car. With the numerous trips to hospitals across the country for my arm, my partner's systemic lupus erythematosus and plus my son's reflex anoxic seizures and my daughter's issue with only having one kidney, it is cheaper than using unsubsidised public transport by just over £100 a year. That's two weeks' food shopping to us.

Degrading and depressing

We have never been on holiday or even a weekend away as a family. My children get those sorts of treats from their grandad and nanny, who work incredibly hard with their own business to make sure they don't go totally without.

Living on benefits is degrading, depressing and there is no room for any luxury of any kind – ever. We wouldn't have had a Christmas dinner last year if it wasn't for help from a local charity.

I spend my spare time helping mistreated social housing tenants living in dilapidated homes, as well as people who need to complain to companies who get nowhere. I am very, very good with legislation and procedural inequality.

I'm not lazy. So I cannot keep quiet when I read the twaddle being published about benefit claimants. There are fraudsters out there, but the system and society in general are targeting the wrong people.

So to all those who think I'm a lazy, fraudulent scrounger, I'll say this. Put your money where your mouth is.

The next time you meet someone who is on disability allowance, or claiming in some other way, ask yourself if you really have the right to sit in judgement because they are a nice, easy target.

Someone on Twitter said they would happily give up work and stay in bed for £11,000. Go on, then. Try to maintain any kind of lifestyle.

This isn't living, it is surviving.

This article was first published by MSE
www.moneysavingexpert.com/news/reclaim/2012/02/im-on-
benefits-but-dont-call-me-a-scrounger

"They should have personal masseuses"

Three days in the classroom gave comedian Rhod Gilbert a new-found respect for teachers

Spending three days in a primary school for my television programme Rhod Gilbert's Work Experience was among the most inspiring things I have ever done.

What's key to teaching is the element that I loved the most: imparting knowledge and information to the children, watching them learn and, you hope, becoming a force for good in their lives. It was incredibly inspiring, moving and the most wonderful privilege.

I got a taste of it for just a few days - after a very short period, kids were coming up to me and saying the most moving things, the most inspirational things, about the impact I'd had on them. And that was me just dicking about and having fun with them, giving them time, listening. I can only imagine what it's like to teach them for years. It must be mind-blowing.

In my time at the school, I learned that it is impossible to overestimate the value teachers have in our society. It's priceless. But, amazingly, teachers are fairly poorly respected. These people are shaping the next generation, they are having a massive influence on what society will be like in five, 10, 15 years' time. It's as much down to them as it is to parents.

Yet many teachers I know are tired, stressed, downtrodden, poorly rewarded, overworked, over-examined and league-tabled to within an inch of their lives, and we as a society, as parents, as politicians, have a duty to do something about it.

So I have come up with a radical solution. All teachers should have government-funded personal masseuses, drivers and personal assistants to massage their shoulders on the way to school and rub their feet. All so that, when they go into the classroom, they are excited, motivated and fresh as a daisy. The rest of us should be doing this...or, at least, the rest of us in society who are paid pointlessly large sums of money for doing sod all.

The teachers at the school where I was placed were committed down to their very last drop of energy and passion. They were phenomenal and the school was awesome. Despite the piles of paperwork, bureaucracy and nonsense that seem to do little more than destroy teachers, they were still incredibly enthusiastic and undaunted - a testament to how passionate they are about their jobs.

SOME ISSUES:

Do you think teachers have a lot of stress in their job?

Do students and parents consider this?

What can people do to help teachers deal with the stress of their job?

Would you like to be a teacher? Why?

Selected from Complete Issues:
Teacher talk
Fact File 2012 p28

Teachers are tired, stressed, downtrodden, poorly rewarded, overworked, over-examined and league-tabled to within an inch of their lives

Then, a jam sandwich was considered two of your five a day and schools were made up of teachers in classrooms, blackboards and rows of kids slumped over desks, learning by rote.

In Monnow Primary, near Newport, South Wales, where I was based for the programme, it's all independent "zones", including the "multimedia zone" and the "thinking zone". For example, they didn't do maths in the classroom, they did it in a forest. It was like something from The Mighty Boosh.

But then, over the three days, I saw how the school's methods engaged the kids and how they loved it, and how much fun they had while they were learning. I became convinced that teaching has really improved in terms of learning through play.

I dicked around a lot when I was in school. I wasn't bad, but I just wasn't interested. It wasn't my teachers, it was just

The teachers at the school where I was placed were committed down to their very last drop of energy and passion

But my time in school wasn't as simple as me walking in to the staffroom and falling in love with the profession. The first day I spent just taking the mick because of all the happy-clappy, modern, funky teaching methods.

The main reason for my reaction was that it was so different from when I was at school in the 1970s.

me. If we'd had the teaching methods I saw in this school, I would certainly have been more engaged.

I was only at Monnow for three days, but I'm going to go back there and help out, because I felt like I had an impact. It was sensational. The best thing I've ever done.

TES magazine, 11 May 2012

SEX EDUCATION MUST BE MORE THAN PLASTIC PENISES AND CONDOMS

British sex education is no better than a set of colourless Ikea assembly instructions for some flat-pack furniture. It needs a full overhaul, forcing teachers to move beyond the biology onto the emotional and physical realities of sex, writes Alice Sholl.

I remember my first experience with a condom. It was a year before my GCSE exams: my classmates and I were just leaving a Citizenship class, and we were chewing on them like gum. They were mint flavoured. We had just been taught how to put condoms on plastic penises as an introduction to our sexual lives – as if the Government had said: "Go on, you young rascals, go fornicate, because now we've told you you can."

But this is when most of us were 15. For some of us, condoms were old news, a thing they had been putting to use for years already. An assignment expected to cause embarrassment and surprise was met with boredom. The lesson was pretty much useless, and far too late.

When people my age, in their early twenties, look back on our sex education in school, it is only as a source of jokes. Not because it involved pictures of naked bodies with genitals, but because of just how useless it was. By the end of it we could draw accurate diagrams of every day of the menstrual cycle, but were never told where to buy tampons. We knew to use condoms, but had no idea what to do if one of our friends did fall pregnant.

SOME ISSUES:

Do you think sex education in school is adequate?

Whose responsibility is it to make sure young people receive the right amount of sex education?

Is it relevant to you and your generation?

Should schools teach you about relationships and emotions?

Our sex education was only a source of jokes. Not because it involved pictures of naked bodies with genitals, but because of just how useless it was.

In a recent review, the Department for Education said that Personal, Social, Health and Economic Education (PSHE), along with its Sex and Relationships Education component, is to remain a non-statutory subject. This can lead to what little sex education there is being essentially a biology lesson; with the focus being on sperm-meets-egg, STIs and HIV. Young adults will be taught the mechanics, but possibly nothing of relationships or emotional consequences. They could leave school believing that sex organs aren't attached to human beings at all.

Leaving young adults to figure it out alone can have a real impact on their lives. The UK has the highest teen pregnancy rate in western Europe, as we are constantly reminded by the media, and an alarming rate of teenagers cannot recognise abuse and rape – only 37 per cent of young adults say they would

as "a kind of advertising manual rather than a proper sex and relationship education", and he was right. Young adults are given advice comparable to the wordless instructions that come with an Ikea flat-pack item. The comedy Swedish cartoon man miserably struggling under a chrome shelf unit isn't very helpful in furnishing a room, but he might provide better sex education advice. At least he could use a series of dramatic arm gestures to warn young adults about the emotional implications of their actions.

In the House of Commons in January Jim Shannon MP of Strangford argued against sex education for young children, and said "so much for an age of innocence". No doubt you're laughing too – an "age of innocence"? One in three children aged 10 have viewed pornography on the internet (as I had). You can find endless similar statistics.

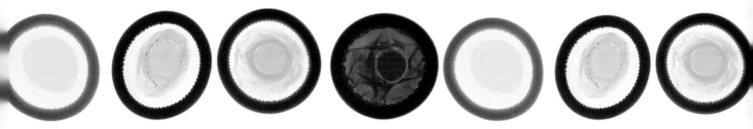

By the end of it we could draw accurate diagrams of every day of the menstrual cycle, but were never told where to buy tampons.

assume their partner does not want to have sex with them if they are crying. Regardless of statistics, any teenager knows young adults start dealing with STIs, abortion and abuse within relationships from a younger age than adults would like to believe. So it should be beyond dispute that every teenager has access to information on how to have healthy relationships and sex lives; and this access is currently at risk.

In the January review of PSHE, Chris Bryant, MP for Rhondda, described current sex education

The fact is, children and young adults will be exposed to sex, and you can't stop it. Really, you can't. But you can provide them with the guidance to help them through it. Young adults must be given sex education, and it must cover relationships and emotions, not just the biology. Yes, and they must be given condoms, whether they choose to use them, or chew on them.

The Daily Telegraph, 26 April 2013
© Telegraph Media Group Limited 2013

We knew to use condoms, but had no idea what to do if one of our friends did fall pregnant.

SCHOOL FEES BUY MORE THAN GOOD GRADES

PRIVATE EDUCATION GIVES PUPILS A PRECIOUS GIFT: CONFIDENCE

ROWAN PELLING

SOME ISSUES:

Do you think a private school education is worth parents selling their house for?

Aside from grades, what do you think a private school can offer pupils?

Would you prefer to attend a private or a state school?

What would you choose for your children?

Selected from Complete Issues:
Closed shop
Fact File 2010 p182

A relative who worked for a London charity once told me how she came across a family of seven, all squeezed into a one-bedroom flat. This was far from your standard Dickensian tale of woe, however, since the parents' reduced circumstances were a direct result of their decision to sell their home and possessions to fund their children through private school. On skid row, with no assets, they lived on porridge, but qualified for bursaries and book grants, and had ensured, by the most tenacious measures imaginable, that their children had as top flight an education as their own.

I have never been able to decide whether this couple deserved an award for an outstanding act of parental sacrifice, or whether they should be carted off to see a shrink; but the last week was one that might make many people believe they were on the right side of lunacy. First, a study led by an academic at Durham University concluded that the entry policies of the elite Russell Group of universities were skewed in favour of privately educated children [*The Russell Group represents 24 leading UK universities including Oxford and Cambridge.*] Compounding those findings was the news that half of the Russell Group had reported a drop in the proportion of places awarded to state school applicants (presumably because of the aforementioned bias). On top of that, the singer Sandie Shaw declared that she would never have succeeded in today's cultural climate, because she didn't go to public school. And there was I, rashly thinking that becoming a pop star was about the only sure-fire way, outside football, for a working-class kid to make their millions, especially now that reality TV is dominated by Made in Chelsea.

THE PARENTS' REDUCED CIRCUMSTANCES WERE A DIRECT RESULT OF THEIR DECISION TO SELL THEIR HOME AND POSSESSIONS TO FUND THEIR CHILDREN THROUGH PRIVATE SCHOOL.

When you read such stories, the notion of flogging your chattels to put your children through Marlborough doesn't look quite so daft, especially when you consider what that course did for the Middleton sisters in terms of social mobility. In fact, it doesn't take much more angst for the typical middle-class parent to conclude they're depriving their children by not downgrading to a shed and educating them privately. I can't help noting that in Cambridge, where I live, many Left-leaning academics don't fret for a second over buying an elite education. The fact their offspring will learn Latin, Greek and modern languages makes the choice a no-brainer. They know better than anyone that no child, however brilliant, can make it through the Oxbridge entrance process without the right tools.

Michael Gove underlined this point this week when he said state schools' failure to make greater inroads into the Russell Group was partly down to poor choices at A-level. Pupils who aren't advised to study rigorous, traditional subjects at sixth form can be disadvantaged; the student whose fourth A star is in media studies won't stand a chance against the one who has that extra grade in further maths. On top of all that, state-school applicants will almost certainly be a zillion times less prepared for the rigours of the Oxbridge interview process than their public-school peers.

This was brought home to me when a friend came to lunch with me in Cambridge last weekend, while his shy 16-year-old daughter attended an access day at one of the science faculties. My friend said that if his child were to be offered a place at Cambridge, she would become the first child from her comprehensive to achieve this feat. The biggest threat to her chances was not poor teaching (she has a raft of A stars) but her fear of putting herself forward. She's not alone. Every don in Cambridge tells me that the biggest bar to increasing state-school access is pupils' reluctance to apply in the first place.

There's much disapproving talk nowadays of over-confident children behaving with "entitlement", but no recognition that less privileged students may need to borrow a little of that swagger. When I look around it seems that it's the entitled who will inherit the earth. David Cameron and Boris Johnson could not have got where they are today without feeling absolutely assured, throughout their lives, of their ability, if not right, to take command. Ditto the Milibands, who obtained similar poise via Camden's intellectual elite. Margaret Thatcher felt entitled too, because that's what a good grammar school did for a girl – but what the comprehensives that replaced so many of them often failed to replicate.

Indeed, I find it ironic that the very quality I like most about my sons' excellent, inclusive local primary school – what you might term an absolute lack of entitlement – may not be valued sufficiently in the outside world. Because what private schools really put a price on is something more nebulous than A grades: it's their ability to endow pupils with an apparently effortless air of success. The canniest state establishments have learnt to emulate this bravado; when the others follow suit, fewer parents will feel compelled to flog their home for fees.

Daily Telegraph, 30 March 2013
© *Telegraph Media Group Limited 2013*

WHAT PRIVATE SCHOOLS REALLY PUT A PRICE ON IS THEIR ABILITY TO ENDOW PUPILS WITH AN APPARENTLY EFFORTLESS AIR OF SUCCESS.

Oxford and Cambridge universities need to tackle race issues head-on

Ignoring under-representation and exclusion isn't good enough for universities that pride themselves on being among the best

Azita Chellappoo

The problem:

An investigation by the Guardian found a disturbing difference in admissions to Oxford university between different ethnic groups.

For example more than half of white students with three A*s were awarded a place in 2010 and 2011.

However, in contrast, only one in three Chinese or Asian students and fewer than one in four black applicants with the same grades were offered places.

SOME ISSUES:

Why do you think universities like Oxford and Cambridge have less racial integration than other universities?

How can students help to tackle this?

And what should the universities do?

On my first day at Oxford University I went to pick up my college welcome pack; there were two piles, one for domestic and one for international students. I asked for one (in my London accent, as that's where I've lived all my life), and got the immediate response: "Are you from India?" I am not from India, neither are my parents or grandparents. The implication that being brown and being British are somehow incompatible is something I was not a stranger to, but it hadn't lost its power to affect me.

You don't need statistics to see that Oxford has a problem when it comes to ethnic minorities. In the hundred-strong intake for my subject, biological sciences, there were two black people, and to the best of my knowledge there were no black students in my year in my college.

Looking around, from those I met at interviews to students in my lectures and the lecturers themselves, there was a noticeable lack of people who weren't white. While my time at Oxford was largely positive, and I had good working relationships with my tutors and fellow students, I couldn't help but be conscious of the difference between their skin and mine – something I hadn't felt at my London school.

Part of the reason for this under-representation is certainly class. This week's data showing that ethnic minority students who get 3 A*s at A-level are less likely to receive offers doesn't surprise me. The Oxford interview process, by its very nature, favours those with the confidence and preparation that comes with going to a top private school. Such schools know how to play the Oxbridge game; they know what interviewers want, and train students to give it to them. As ethnic minorities are under-represented at these schools, so they are also under-represented at Oxford.

I was lucky enough to go to a private school – although not a particularly impressive one – where I was given some help and knew others who had gone through the process. I have

Race issues are never tackled head-on but instead brushed under the carpet.

anecdotal evidence for the impact of the school from one friend, who applied twice to Cambridge, first successfully with the support of the school (but due to complex circumstances could not take up the offer) and then without. They found the second time round much more difficult (even with the help from the year before) and failed to gain a place.

Students often lack awareness of racial issues, and this goes unchallenged

Explaining away this under-representation with reasons other than racism does not get Oxford off the hook, however. The lack of ethnic minority students and staff creates its own problems. On a personal level, it can make ethnic minority students feel uncomfortable and "other". In a meeting with my Scandinavian supervisor and two other students, one student asked if another person mentioned was Scandinavian (as they themselves were by descent),

as that would mean they could "all be Scandinavians together". There was no reaction, positive or negative, from the supervisor. I sat there, as the only non-white person in the meeting, feeling incredibly conscious of that fact.

It also means that students often lack awareness of racial issues, and this goes unchallenged. I have seen Oxford students with yellow-painted faces for their Chinese-origin friend's birthday, because "this is the one day she allows us to be racist". Unpacking that statement could fill a doctoral thesis. This feedback loop means that ethnic minorities are discouraged from applying and are more likely to have negative experiences when they do attend, which paves the way for insidious racism borne out of ignorance and lack of interaction.

The usual reactions to the problem of under-representation are to dismiss or ignore it. Bringing up the question of racial bias at Oxford does not mean accusing tutors or staff of racism. It does not mean that racism is the primary causal factor in the under-representation of ethnic minorities. It does not mean that this is a problem confined to Oxbridge, or that it is even the worst in these places. What we have is a system where, in the universities that pride themselves on being among the best in the world, race issues are never tackled head-on but instead brushed under the carpet.

If the goal is better representation of ethnic minorities, pointing to the effect of class and leaving it there is not going to help. If the goal is to recruit the best students and get the best out of them, hand-waving about policies of inclusion is not good enough. We have to push for the world we want to live in, and the first step is recognising that we have a problem.

The Guardian, 28 February 2013
© Guardian News and Media Ltd 2013

Environmental issues

WHAT are we WORRIED about?

CO_2

Scientists believe in climate change so why doesn't everyone?

SOME ISSUES:

Could scientists themselves do more to make their voices heard?

Is it too late to change the way we live, in order to save the planet?

How should the media balance their reporting of complicated issues like this?

Selected from Complete Issues:
If climate change didn't exist, would we have to invent it?
Essential Articles 13 p70

In May 2013 a group of scientists published their own paper in which they reviewed thousands of other academic papers. Their paper confirmed something they already knew but which many members of the public still did not accept. They proved that the overwhelming majority of scientists believe that climate change is occurring and that it is caused by human activity.

Their analysis looked at the work of 29,000 scientists and showed that 97.1% agreed that global warming was caused by human behaviour. Only 0.7% of the articles actually disputed or opposed this view; that's just 83 articles out of the thousands studied. In the remaining 2.2% of the papers the opinion was unclear.

According to John Cook of the University of Queensland, who led the survey, the results prove that there is a strong scientific agreement about the cause of climate change yet this is not reflected in the views of the public. "There is a gaping chasm between the actual consensus and the public perception," he said.

Certainly research in the United States seems to suggest a gulf. While 67% of Americans agree there is solid evidence that the earth's average temperature has been getting warmer over the past few decades only 42% say this warming is mostly caused by human activity, such as burning fossil fuels. There is more public disagreement over scientific opinion: asked whether they think scientists agree that the earth is warming mostly because of human activity; 45% of the public say scientists do agree while 43% say they do not.

So how has this public uncertainty come about? According to the report, those industries who would be affected by measures to halt climate change have made forceful efforts to undermine opinions and research. These industries also tried to give the impression that the matter was still being debated by scientists. By giving a platform to the small number of dissenting voices they made it look as if there was controversy where in fact there was mainly consensus.

Within the media, too, the practice of creating balance by allowing equal space to both sides of an argument has meant that the voices of the vast majority and of a very small minority were given equal weight.

Why does this matter? The authors of the report believe that if people knew the strength of scientific agreement that could change public opinion and attitudes. And if public attitudes change, then political action becomes more likely. But "Scientists agree" does not make headlines.

So, if we – or the news media – are not worrying sufficiently about global warming, what are we worrying about?

On Friday 10 May 2013 new figures were published showing that carbon dioxide levels had reached 400 parts per million in our atmosphere. The last time this happened was several million years ago. Scientists saw this as a milestone, a warning that global warming caused by CO_2 emissions from human activity was increasing to the point of no return.

So, on the day that we were warned that unless we radically changed our energy demands we would return the planet to a prehistoric state, what was on the front pages of UK newspapers? The Daily Telegraph featured MP expenses scandals, the Guardian highlighted offshore tax havens for the richest people, the Independent ran with funding chaos in the NHS and the Times featured 'Archbishop in cover up over abuse scandal.'

All these are obviously important issues – though it is questionable whether they rate higher than the destruction of the planet. Meanwhile the popular tabloid press covered the new manager at Manchester United (The Sun and the Daily Star), immigration (the Daily Express) and tax dodgers (the Daily Mail). The Daily Mirror's huge headline and picture featured 'Corrie Kev's new love'.

What are we worried about? To judge by these headlines – money, sex, football, immigration, TV soaps and the NHS. The fate of our planet? Not really.

Source: Various

GREENLAND REAPS BENEFITS OF GLOBAL WARMING

By Alistair Scrutton

On the Arctic Circle, a chef is growing the kind of vegetables and herbs – potatoes, thyme, tomatoes, green peppers – more fitting for a suburban garden in a temperate zone than a land of Northern Lights, glaciers and musk oxen.

Some Inuit hunters are finding reindeer fatter than ever thanks to more grazing on this frozen tundra, and for some, there is no longer a need to trek hours to find wild herbs.

Welcome to climate change in Greenland, where locals say longer and warmer summers mean the country can grow the kind of crops unheard of years ago.

"Things are just growing quicker," said Kim Ernst, the Danish chef of Roklubben restaurant, nestled by a frozen lake near a former Cold War-era U.S. military base.

"Every year we try new things," said Ernst, who even managed to grow a handful of strawberries that he served to some surprised Scandinavian royals. "I first came here in 1999 and no-one would have dreamed of doing this. But now the summer days seem warmer, and longer."

It was minus 20 degrees Centigrade in March but the sun was out and the air was still, with an almost spring feel. Ernst showed his greenhouse and an outdoor winter garden which in a few months may sprout again.

Hundreds of miles south, some farmers now produce hay, and sheep farms have increased in size. Some supermarkets in the capital Nuuk sell locally grown vegetables during the summer.

Major commercial crop production is still in its infancy. But it is a sign of changes here that Greenland's government set up a commission this year to study how a changing climate may help farmers increase agricultural production and replace expensive imported foods.

Change is already underway. Potatoes grown commercially in southern Greenland reached over 100 tonnes in 2012, double that of 2008. Vegetable production in the region may double this year compared with 2012, according to government data.

Some politicians hope global warming will allow this country, a quarter the size of the United States, to reduce its dependency on former colonial master Denmark for much of its food as political parties push for full independence.

Greenland, which is self-governing aside from defence and security, depends on an annual grant from Denmark of around $600 million, or half the island's annual budget. But the thawing of its enormous ice sheets have seen a boost in mining and oil exploration, as well as an interest in agriculture.

SOME ISSUES:

Is Greenland getting a benefit from global warming?

Would other countries share Greenland's view of climate change?

"I expect a lot of development in farming sheep and agriculture due to global warming," said Prime Minister Kuupik Kleist, whose government set up the commission. "It may become an important supplement to our economy."

Locals love recounting how Erik the Red first arrived in the southern fjords here in the 10th century and labelled this ice-covered island "Greenland" to entice others to settle. There is evidence that the climate was warmer then, allowing Viking settlements to grow crops for five centuries before mysteriously dying out.

FROM COWS TO CROPS

The scale of this new agriculture is tiny. There are just a few dozen sheep farms in southern Greenland, where most of the impact of climate change can be seen. Cows may number less than a hundred. But with 57,000 mostly Inuit human inhabitants, the numbers to feed are also small.

"You need to put this into perspective. We used to be high Arctic and now we are more sub Arctic," Kenneth Hoegh, an agronomist and former senior government advisor. "But we are still Arctic."

The symbolism is enormous, however, highlighting a changing global climate that has seen temperatures in the Arctic increase by about twice the global average - about 0.8 degrees Celsius since pre-industrial times.

"There are now huge areas in southern Greenland where you can grow things," said Josephine Nymand, a scientist at the Greenland Institute of Natural Resources in Nuuk. "Potatoes have most benefited. Also, cabbage has been very successful."

Sten Erik Langstrup Pedersen, who runs an organic farm in a fjord near Nuuk, first grew potatoes in 1976. Now he can plant crops two weeks earlier in May and harvest three weeks later in October compared with more than a decade ago.

He grows 23 kinds of vegetables, compared with 15 a decade ago, including beans, peas, herbs and strawberries. He says he has sold some strawberries to top restaurants in Copenhagen.

But Pedersen is sceptical about how much it will catch on.

"Greenlanders are impatient. They see a seal and they immediately just want to hunt it. They can never wait for vegetables to grow."

There is still potential. Hoegh estimates Greenland could provide half its food needs from home-grown produce which would be competitive with more expensive Danish imports.

But global change is not all about benefits. While summers are warmer, there is less rain. Some experts say that Greenland could soon need irrigation works - ironic for a country of ice and lakes.

"We have had dry summers for the last few years." said Aqqalooraq Frederiksen, a senior agricultural consultant in south Greenland, who said a late spring last year hurt potato crops.

On the Arctic circle, a flash flood last summer from suspected glacier melt water - which some locals here blamed on warm weather - swept away the only bridge connecting Ernst's restaurant to the airport. It came right in the middle of the tourist season, and the restaurant lost thousands of dollars.

It was an ominous reminder that global warming will bring its problems. Still, for Pedersen and his fjord in Nuuk, the future looks good.

"The hotter, the better," Pedersen said. "For me."

(Additional reporting by Katja Vahl in Nuuk; Editing by Sonya Hepinstall)

Source: Reuters

Imaginative upcycling:

how waste can be made into something wonderful

We live in a throwaway society, a world where we have so much that we can dump our junk and move on - leaving the problem of dealing with the rubbish to some unspecified time in the future.

While the huge quantity of rubbish is a problem, for creative minds it's also an opportunity. All over the world there are initiatives to take items from our rubbish heaps and make them into something fresh new and exciting - 'upcycling' rubbish into desirable furniture and fashion items in the developed world and re-using waste to provide essentials in developing countries.

Scoopa

In the Scoopa project in Greece a group of architects, artists and craftsmen collaborate to manufacture items which have the least possible carbon footprint since they are mainly upcycled from existing items.

"We use discarded components, which may look useless. What is trash to you is a treasure to us and can become part of a creative chain".

They will use anything, any size from a pin to a container. They produce fabulously cool furniture from oil drums or old suitcases, rings made from zips or keyboard letters, lights made from plastic bottles and bags made from old advertising banners.

SOME ISSUES:

Does it really matter how much we waste?

Would knowing something was 'upcycled' make you more likely to buy it or less likely?

How many items that are normally thrown away could you invent a good use for?

Selected from Complete Issues:
Poverty or poison
Essential Articles 12 p74

M&S and Oxfam

In April 2012 Marks and Spencer and Oxfam launched the idea of shwopping. Shoppers were rewarded with money-off vouchers for donating old M&S clothes to Oxfam. In M&S stores there are 'Shwop drops' for donating clothes from any manufacturer. Donated materials are also used to make new clothes. The first product was a ladies coat made from 'shwopped' wool. The idea is clearly popular, over 3 million items of clothing have been donated to be re-sold, re-used or re-cycled by Oxfam.

Elvis & Kresse

In London, partnership Elvis & Kresse have a mission: "We dream of a time without landfill, when everything is recycled or composted. Between now and then we know there are far too many incredible materials that will either languish under ground or suffer the indignity of incineration; when that happens we lose, we lose quality, narrative, and the opportunity to do something great."

And here is that something great: they take fire hoses from the London Fire Brigade, which would otherwise go into landfill, and make highly desirable belts, bags, wallets and even guitar straps. The hoses can have been on active duty for up to 25 years, fighting fires and saving lives, but the material retains its resilience. Kresse had the initial idea in 2005, by 2010 they were using all of the London Fire Brigade's redundant hose, 10 tonnes per year. As well as upcycling the hoses and saving them from landfill, they give 50% of the profit on this range to the Fire Fighters charity.

Cateura Orchestra of Recycled Instruments

The 30 schoolchildren who make up the orchestra are the sons and daughters of recyclers. Their parents scratch a living by separating out bits of aluminium and plastic from the waste of the city of Asuncion, capital of Paraguay.

Favio Chávez, the conductor of the orchestra, was a technician at the Cateura landfill site but also conducted a youth orchestra in his home town. When he was asked by the recyclers to teach their children he willingly took on the task but there was an immediate problem. The children needed to practise but could never afford instruments. Even to loan them instruments would have been difficult.

"A violin is worth more than a recycler's house," says Chávez. "We couldn't give a child a formal instrument as it would have put him in a difficult position. The family may have looked to sell or trade it."

So he began, literally, to dig out materials: an oven tray to form the body of a violin, an oil drum for a cello, old bits of wood to sculpt into the necks.

Being part of the orchestra has given these slum children an experience of travel and acclaim but, according to Chavez, it also gives them an ability to plan ahead. For people in abject poverty it is difficult to think beyond the immediate day to day needs. Chavez believes that playing in the orchestra can allow the children to see beyond the horizons of the landfill site. While shaping his landfill instruments he is also shaping lives.

"There were a lot of drugs, alcohol, violence, child labor – a lot of situations that you wouldn't think are favorable for kids to learn values. However, they have a spot in the orchestra.

Like an island within the community, a place where they can develop these values.

We've seen cases where parents with addiction problems have quit taking drugs to go to their kid's concerts. And in a lot of cases, the parents have gone back to finish school because their kids are being seen all over and they think, 'They are going forward. I want to, as well.'

They are not only changing their lives but the lives of their families and their community."

– Favio Chavez
Orchestra Director

www.kickstarter.com/projects/405192963/landfill-harmonic-inspiring-dreams-one-note-at-a-t

Sources: Various

Family &
relationships

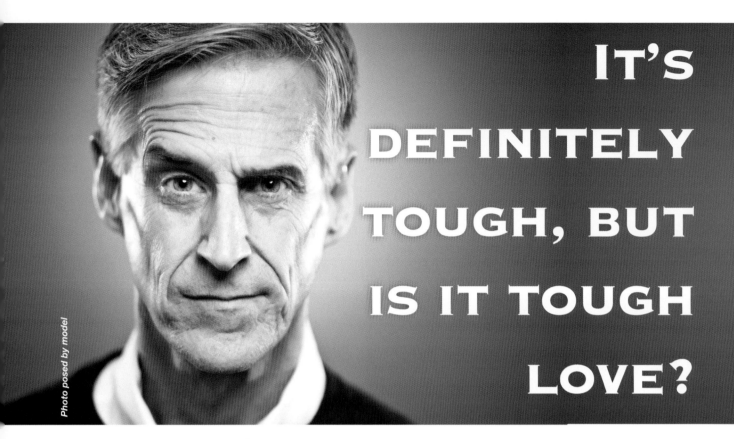

Photo posed by model

IT'S DEFINITELY TOUGH, BUT IS IT TOUGH LOVE?

A FATHER'S BITTER EMAIL TO HIS GROWN-UP CHILDREN:

SOME ISSUES:

Should a parent still have a say in the life of a child even when that 'child' is an adult?

Do children have a duty to make use of opportunities their parents give them?

Is this email a kick up the backside or a slap in the face for the children?

How should they react?

How would you?

Nick Crews, a former Royal Navy officer, was so disappointed in the way his three grown up children, a son and two daughters, were running their lives that he wrote them an email setting out his complaints and saying he did not want to hear from them until they had changed their ways. The email was then published in national newspapers.

The email, which begins *"Dear all three"* was in response to a *"crop of whinges and rotten news"* from his children, who are aged between 35 and 40, who he feels have not made enough of their opportunities. The father pulls no punches from the very beginning:

"It is obvious that none of you has the faintest notion of the bitter disappointment each of you has in your own way dished out to us."

He complains about their failed marriages and goes on to list the ways in which he feels his children have failed:

BY COMPARISON WITH OTHERS

"We are constantly regaled with chapter and verse of the happy, successful lives of the families of our friends and relatives and being asked of news of our own children and grandchildren. I wonder if you realise how we feel – we have nothing to say which reflects any credit on you or us."

AS PROVIDERS

"Having done our best – probably misguidedly – to provide for our children, we naturally hoped to see them in turn... provide happy and stable homes for their own children.

Fulfilling careers based on your educations would have helped — but as yet none of you is what I would confidently term properly self-supporting... Each of you is well able to earn a comfortable living and provide for your children, yet each of you has contrived to avoid even moderate achievement. Far from your children being able to rely on your provision,

IF YOU THINK I HAVE BEEN UNFAIR IN WHAT I HAVE SAID, BY ALL MEANS TRY TO PERSUADE ME TO CHANGE MY MIND. BUT YOU WON'T DO IT BY SIMPLY WHINGEING AND SAYING YOU DON'T LIKE IT.

they are faced with needing to survive their introduction to life with you as parents."

AS PARENTS:

He complains that his grandchildren are saddled with parents who don't have *"maturity and sound judgment"* and who make *"hasty, but always in our view, badly judged decisions"* without consulting their own parents for advice: *"None of you has done yourself, or given to us, the basic courtesy to ask us what we think while there was still time finally to think things through."* He mentions *"a decade of deep unhappiness over the fates of our grandchildren ... these lovely little people being so woefully let down by you, their parents...*

Enough!"

FINALLY HE THROWS DOWN THE CHALLENGE:

"I want to hear no more from any of you until, if you feel inclined, you have a success or an achievement or a REALISTIC plan for the

support and happiness of your children to tell me about ... If you think I have been unfair in what I have said, by all means try to persuade me to change my mind. But you won't do it by simply whingeing and saying you don't like it. You'll have to come up with meaty reasons to demolish my points and build a case for yourself. If that isn't possible, or you simply can't be bothered, then I rest my case.

I am bitterly, bitterly disappointed.

Dad"

Mr Crews received support from other parents who said, 'I feel exactly the same about my children.' Or, 'You've said what I wish I'd said a long time ago.' and from journalists. For example, Simon Warr, wrote in the East Anglian Daily Times:

"He was right to be honest. He and his wife had gone that extra yard to ensure all three had as supportive and loving an upbringing as they, as parents, could possibly afford them. Their children now had a duty to respect this by being good

parents themselves and by carving out successful careers."

Even one of his daughters felt that his email was justified and it was she who asked if it could be published to help raise interest in a self-help book she was translating. Her brother and sister, however, have not spoken to their father since they received the email.

Nick Crews himself has said that he regrets that the email became so public, but does not regret what he said

"It said what I truly felt; and if I've learnt one thing in life, it is that you have to be true to yourself."

His own interpretation of the email is different from at least two of his children:

"I was trying to express my frustration at these wonderful grown-ups who had yet to make the best of what they had. They have read the criticism, but not seen the enduring love through the lines."

Tough love? Or just tough?

Sources: Various

Think you can't run away from your problems? I'm living proof YOU CAN!

Bundled into a car in the dead of night, Christi Daugherty set off for a new life with her mother, brother and budgie – leaving her father behind

BY CHRISTI DAUGHERTY

SOME ISSUES:

Were the family right to run away from an abusive father or could they have done something else?

Why do you think their life was so much better once they made the move?

Why might this have strengthened the writer's relationship with her mother?

Selected from Complete Issues:
'I witnessed terrible things'
Essential Articles 13 p79
Safe house
Fact File 2012 p56

'Wake up.' My mother is shaking me roughly. It's dark. I sit up in bed with a gasp. My new alarm-clock blinks at me from the top of the dresser. 1am.

She flicks on the light as I squint up at her, bewildered. She's fully dressed, her thick, dark hair neatly styled. There's a suitcase on the floor – it wasn't there when I went to bed.

'Get dressed.' Her voice is brittle. She's starting to scare me. 'I need you to pack this bag with all the things you'll need for a few weeks. Dress for warm weather.' I'm baffled. It's late August in Montana, near the Canadian border, and autumn has already arrived – it's freezing outside.

Her hands are trembling and tension fairly crackles in the air around her. Even at 13 I know better than to argue. When I drag my suitcase downstairs 10 minutes later, my seven-year-old brother, Joe, is already strapped into the back seat of the car. My budgie, Pumpkin, tweets nervously from her cage on the seat beside him.

My mother's best friend is standing next to her. I cannot imagine what she's doing here – she lives 15 miles away. 'You ready for a drive?' she asks brightly, as if it were a sunny afternoon and we were going on a picnic. 'You're going to have to keep your mother awake. Sing songs and talk really loud.' I glare at her with baleful suspicion.

Every adult in the world has gone crazy. Then we're in the car, driving through empty streets. Behind me, Joe has already fallen asleep. My mother looks pale. Her hands grip the steering-wheel hard.

Only when the town's lights fade into darkness behind us does she tell me what's happening. We are running away. We're going back to Texas, where we are from, to start a new life as far away from my father as we can get. My heart pounds with excitement. At last we will be free.

Dad is one of those men of whom people used to say, 'He's got a helluva temper.' Today they'd call him abusive. He beat my mother every time she upset him. He beat us, too, but less often. His new-found Christian fundamentalism did nothing to curb his anger. When my parents divorced I thought it would end but it didn't – he broke into our house.

I'm dizzy at the thought of getting away, but first we have to get across the state line. My father has an injunction to prevent my mother from taking us out of the state. As soon as he realises we're gone he'll call the police. Or, worse, he'll come after us himself.

The distance from Helena, Montana, to Dallas, Texas, is 1,670 miles. It took us 35 hours and, by the end of it, everything had changed. I was no longer a selfish 13-year-old child. Instead I was a young woman, my mother's partner-in-crime, a whizz at map-reading, child-wrangling and cop-spotting. Thelma to her Louise.

Every moment of that drive is seared on my memory. Lying to Joe that we're going on holiday. Dodging the suspicious gaze of a police officer in a Wyoming petrol station, sick with fear. Getting lost in the New Mexico desert. Cheering when we passed the Welcome to Texas sign.

Even after we settled in Houston things never went back to the way they'd been; I was never a child again. My mother and I made decisions about everything together – from what to have for dinner to where we should live. When Joe was old enough we decided as a collective. We were poor but safe, and I'd never been happier.

Photos posed by models

Dad is one of those men of whom people used to say, 'He's got a helluva temper.' Today they'd call him abusive.

I've often wondered if that journey impacted on my later life. I have run away many times – from jobs, boyfriends and boredom.

I moved to England in 2000 after a bad break-up in New Orleans – my longest run ever. Until I got married in 2007 I'd never lived in the same house for more than two years. I never own – always rent. 'I don't like to be pinned down,' I hear myself say, and I wonder why I'm saying it.

They claim you can't run away from your troubles but I just don't believe that's true. I'm living proof that you can.

Legacy, by CJ Daugherty, is published by Atom at £6.99

The Daily Telegraph, 4 February 2013
© The Telegraph Media Group 2013

I was no longer a selfish 13-year-old child. Instead I was a young woman, my mother's partner-in-crime

Virginia Ironside's Dilemmas:

Our dad abandoned the family. How can we forgive him?

This reader's father left the family for another woman last year. Now mum's taken him back, but his children are in a less forgiving mood

Dear Virginia,

I'm 15 and last year my dad left us to go off with another woman. It made us all so unhappy but in a way it was a relief when all the rows stopped. My younger brother and I took our mum's side and we didn't want to see him again. We'd moved into a smaller home, and things were just starting to be OK again and mum had got a job and we were starting to be happy again, when dad asked to come back. Mum took him back at once, and forgave him, but we just can't. We hate him for what he did. I feel so let down. What can I do?

Yours sincerely, Sonia (15)

Virginia Says...

What I want to know is: Have you told your father how you feel? I imagine that before your mum took him back, they had some proper conversations about what had happened. Presumably he didn't just walk back in. No doubt she explained how betrayed she'd felt, he apologised and was bitterly remorseful, and he assured her it would never happened again. They might have tried to wipe the slate clean and build up a new relationship from scratch.

But, as you've pointed out, he's forgotten about one thing: his children. Or so it seems.

Now, it could be that he thinks that since you thought so little of him to start with, your feelings towards him haven't changed. It could be that he thinks, perhaps because you're an undemonstrative family, that whether he's there or not doesn't make a pin of difference to you. Maybe – and this is a real possibility – he's actually frightened of discussing what's happened with you because he knows how angry you'll be. Or maybe he actually returned because he missed not just your mum, but you two.

SOME ISSUES:

Do you think that Sonia's mum was right to take her partner back?

Do you think Sonia should be more forgiving?

Can you understand why Sonia and her brother might feel this way?

What do you think they should do?

I think it's a lot to ask for you to have a conversation with your father. I think it would demand a maturity beyond your years – but if you felt you could have a proper discussion, without getting too emotional and accusatory, then by all means initiate it.

But I don't see why you shouldn't tell your mother how you feel. It was her decision to have him back, after all, and she should have perhaps made it one of the conditions of his return that he would have a long talk with you and your brother about what had happened.

It sounds as if you're not just angry at his causing so many rows to start with, and angry with him for leaving, but also angry with apparently being side-lined in all the discussions about whether he returned home or not, as if your feelings simply didn't count.

Join forces with your brother – two are always stronger than one – and ask your mother to sort this out on your behalf. And tell her you feel upset that she took a unilateral decision in allowing your father home without consulting you two. And don't leave it open-ended. Tell her what you want to make things better. Insist on having a proper talk with your dad, after he's been primed by your mum, and an acknowledgement, from him that you two have been almost irrevocably hurt by his behaviour.

After what's happened I doubt it'll ever be the perfect family – and remember that few families are perfect, when you scratch the surface – but it could be lot better than it is now.

Readers say...

Learn from this

Your parents have made a massive mistake one way or the other, either by splitting up in the first place or by subsequently getting back together. My family set-up was very similar and believe me, the difficulties you overcome now will make you more resilient in the future. Most importantly, learn from what is happening all around you and don't repeat their mistakes.

Zoe, by email

Let him know

It's understandable that you feel betrayed. You now need to be very careful and open both eyes wide to human nature. Your mother wants him back and you have to accept this. Hate is natural but ultimately destructive. My suggestion is that you ask for a specific time to sit and talk to your father. Say exactly how you feel – directly to him. Don't bottle it up. Don't lie awake at night thinking hateful thoughts – get it out in the open.

Your parents' marriage might get stronger and survive this betrayal but it might not. Whatever you do, don't start living off this hate and upset that you feel. Be bigger than this situation. Your father is still your father; tell him how you feel.

Maureen, by email

© The Independent, 7 January 2013
www.independent.co.uk

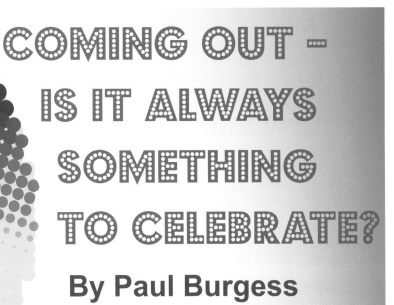

COMING OUT – IS IT ALWAYS SOMETHING TO CELEBRATE?

By Paul Burgess

POSITIVE ROLE MODELS ARE SUCH AN IMPORTANT PART OF OUR LIVES. ALL OF US.

Whether male, female, or trans, young or old. Whether gay, bi, straight, or any of the seemingly ever growing list of identities that fall in between.

Role models can be life changing for some people.

But, and here's the big question, should we always celebrate those who come out late in life? Are they really our best example for young LGBT people everywhere? I mean, what exactly are we celebrating?

Are we revelling in the fact that somebody hid themselves away for many, many years, before realising that they couldn't do it anymore?

Obviously I'm happy for such people, delighted in fact that they have at last taken the plunge and fully accepted who they are, but what about all that went before the reveal? What of the possible/probable hurt caused to others? The lies obviously told to hide the truth?

Celebrate?

The perfect and perhaps most recent example of this is of course, Gareth Thomas*. Or, to clarify, the LGBT Media handling, of Gareth's story.

WHAT EXACTLY ARE WE CELEBRATING?

ARE WE REVELLING IN THE FACT THAT SOMEBODY HID THEMSELVES AWAY FOR MANY, MANY YEARS, BEFORE REALISING THAT THEY COULDN'T DO IT ANYMORE?

SOME ISSUES:

Do you think it is something to celebrate when someone effectively 'comes out of the closet'?

Do you agree with this writer, that it would be better if people didn't feel they had to hide their sexuality in the first place?

GOOD, STRONG, SOLID, STAND UP MEMBERS OF SOCIETY IN GENERAL, WHO JUST HAPPEN TO BE A PART OF THE LGBT COMMUNITY TOO. THOSE ARE THE POSITIVE ROLE MODELS

We all put him up on a pedestal, the shining example for our LGBT youth.

It must be said though, in all fairness, the documentary recently aired about Gareth and his coming out did indeed touch on the darker side, and the effects on other people. He should be proud of covering that, it was fair, frank and raw.

In general however, why don't we, the LGBT community at large, focus more of our attention on the people who have never been in a closet in the first place? Our community is filled with people like this. Loving couples with kids they have through fostering, adoption or fertility treatments.

Good, strong, solid, stand up members of society in general, who just happen to be a part of the LGBT community too. Those are the positive role models I personally want to see, and that I would like to think young people were seeing, reading about and possibly even interacting with.

Our own media, is all too often filled with scantily clad images of 'gay friendly' sport personalities, TV stars or boy bands. The media in general seems to focus far too much on those who come out late in life, or high profile couples like Elton John and David Furnish and their personal lives, again all too often with a negative spin.

We created this environment. We buy the tickets and fill the stalls, we sit waiting patiently for the circus to begin. We are our very own creation.

They say you can't change what you don't acknowledge. So let's change things a little, shall we? We have the power. We always did.

Paul J Burgess is creator and co-founder of Pink Triangle Theatre

Pink News, 21 February 2013

*Gareth Thomas is a retired Welsh Rugby player who officially announced he was gay in 2009. You can read more about Gareth in 'Time to come out to play?', Essential Articles 14, p166

In a generation, everything has changed for British Muslim women

My mother and I both married men from Pakistan. Both marriages ended in divorce, but their circumstances and our attitudes towards them could not have been more different: it is a sign of how much has changed.

IRNA QURESHI

Attitudes towards divorce are changing among British Muslim women. My mother's generation regarded divorce as immoral, so sustaining a marriage for them was a lifelong project. However, for British educated Muslim women like me, divorce is an entitlement, even within Islamic law.

My mother and I married men from Pakistan. Although our marriages took place thirty years apart, they were only registered under Sharia, or Islamic religious law, in Pakistan. Both our marriages ended in divorce, yet the circumstances and our attitudes couldn't have been more different.

My mother didn't have any say in her divorce. She'd worked as a teacher in Pakistan before she was married off to my father in 1964, then a migrant textile mill worker in Bradford. After 15 years of marriage and three children, my father decided to return to Pakistan alone. A couple of years later, he sent mum the finalised Islamic divorce papers by post. The matter was taken completely out of her hands. She wasn't even consulted. Mum felt so humiliated at the thought of becoming a divorced woman, that she couldn't even bring herself to tell anyone what had happened for months. Mum says she understood that some marriages were not as successful as others, but the notion of her own marriage ending in divorce was inconceivable.

SOME ISSUES:

What do you think has contributed to changing people's attitudes about divorce?

How important is education in changing people's circumstances and opinions?

What role does religion play in people's attitudes and customs?

Why might this change over time and from one generation to another?

Muslim women are also becoming more empowered and ensuring they educate themselves on their religious rights

You'd hear about certain girls who couldn't get along with their in-laws for whatever reason. People would say, "That girl isn't worthy. She couldn't conform." There'd be a hint that the girl had some bad habits, or worse, that she was immoral. But that idea of things finishing altogether – well, that was unthinkable. You never heard about that.

For decades afterwards, mum maintained that a lifelong separation would have served her better than the dishonour of a divorce. It didn't matter that she was better qualified and more articulate in English than her husband. While these skills no doubt enabled her to raise her children alone, she didn't regard herself as empowered. She still viewed divorce as the ultimate curse, something the community would use to judge her character.

It's not that my mother wasn't aware of her religious rights. It's just that in her mind, the moral stigma was greater. She knew that although Islam discourages divorce, the faith does acknowledge that situations may arise when marriage no longer fulfils its purpose. She also knew of several examples in Islamic texts and history which emphasise the woman's right to divorce.

One oft-quoted Hadith, a teaching of the Prophet Muhammad, involves a girl who raised a complaint that her father had given her in marriage against her will. The Prophet told the girl that she was at liberty to choose or reject her husband. The girl chose to stay in the marriage, explaining

It's not that my mother wasn't aware of her religious rights. It's just that in her mind, the moral stigma was greater

Although it is still women that bear the brunt of the burden of shame when it comes to divorce, there is now recognition that the wife isn't automatically at fault if a marriage breaks down

that she had only wanted to know whether women had any rights in the matter.

My mother fell victim to the way in which Sharia law discriminates against gender, by making it much easier for a man to end a marriage. A woman can be divorced if her husband simply pronounces talaq (divorce) three times, although ideally he should not exercise this right without first seeking counsel or negotiating with his wife. However, the practice is frequently abused.

There are ways in which a woman may divorce her husband under Islamic law, although these are more drawn out than the simple pronouncement that men are decreed. At the time of marriage, a woman may ask her husband to delegate the power of pronouncing the divorce to her, thereby giving her the authority to dissolve the marriage contract. What's more, a husband can no longer reclaim this power once he has transferred it to his wife. Since Islam regards marriage as a contractual relationship, a Muslim woman may also protect herself with the equivalent of a prenuptial agreement. She may seek a divorce if any of the agreed conditions are violated. In practice however, attaining such entitlements can be difficult. With many unions still arranged by parents, it can be difficult for the bride to make such demands at the time of marriage, particularly if she is yet to build a rapport with her husband.

The most common method for a woman to seek a divorce is to apply to a Sharia law body, a long and drawn out process, and not without expense. This is the route I took in Pakistan, where my marriage was registered, when I found myself several years into an unhappy marriage. Unlike my mother, divorce to me seemed the natural course of action. Although I was worried about the moral judgement I would draw as a divorcee, my freedom and happiness were ultimately more important. I was simply asserting my right.

I also realised that if my Pakistan-based husband opposed the divorce, it would be up to me to persuade the judge to end the marriage, and for that, I would have to navigate the minefield of the family courts in Rawalpindi. Instead, I set about persuading my husband to grant me a divorce through the Muslim family courts in Rawalpindi, where the marriage had been registered.

Attitudes aren't just changing because British Muslim women are becoming more financially independent. Muslim women are also becoming more empowered and ensuring they educate themselves on their religious rights. Although divorce is deeply discouraged in Islam and seen as the last resort, it is nevertheless halal (permissible) for either the husband or the wife to ask for the marriage to be terminated.

Although it is still women that bear the brunt of the burden of shame when it comes to divorce, there is now recognition that the wife isn't automatically at fault if a marriage breaks down. Moreover, with Muslim matrimonial websites now offering specific dating services for Muslim divorcees, there is also a growing appreciation that there is life and romance beyond divorce.

New Statesman, 15 May 2013

Financial issues

If every man or woman's home is their castle, who cares if it costs £1 to buy?

Grace Dent:

Sometimes, just sometimes, councils do something that makes my heart soar with joy.

There are no magical solutions to our nation's housing problem. No pixie dust to fling that will give every family a front door, a bed per child and a table to have jovial teatimes at. But I can't help thinking that this week's £1 home scheme in Stoke-on-Trent is a step in the right direction.

Stoke-on-Trent's local authority has offered up 35 derelict homes for sale – mainly two-bedroom, terraced properties – for the pocket-friendly sum of £1. The homes, or shells of homes, are one mile from the city centre in the Portland Street area of Cobridge, currently standing boarded up, forgotten, neglected, the roads around a hot spot for fly-tipping. The

corner shop and local pub disappeared in 2009.

Take away the cosmetic problems, however, and what you've got is rows of terraced houses. Like the one I grew up in during the Seventies. We were an army of kids playing day after day in the street on rollerskates and BMXs. Not remotely deluxe, yet secure, with a bed to sleep in, and happy. This shouldn't be an impossible dream for new young families. Every corner of the land has houses standing empty. A similar scheme in Liverpool's Kensington seems so far to be very successful. This is not bulldozing in the name of regeneration, but instead it's a strange, slightly hippie commune vibe mixed with the arch-Tory values of "one's home is one's castle" and "get out and scrub your step". Politically, it's everywhere and I really rather love it.

The rules for the purchase seem refreshingly sensible. If you want to apply for a £1 home, you must have a moderate income or joint income of £18,000 to £25,000 a year. If you have kids, you are allowed to earn up to £30,000. On a salary like this, there is little way one can ever save up a deposit to buy unless you have a rich mummy and daddy who will help. This is very much a scheme to help local families get a leg up onto the property ladder; thus one must have lived in the city for the past three years.

SOME ISSUES:

Do you think more councils should employ this type of scheme?

Who does this scheme benefit?

Is this a good way of dealing with the housing problem?

Are rules about who can buy these homes fair?

Selected from Complete Issues:
Locked out
Fact File 2011 p112

Owning one's own home, and answering to no landlord, is a wholly agreeable state

There have been mumblings about the £1 houses, with claims that they are "patronising" and will only introduce ghettos.

Likewise, property developers can sling their hook, and owning any other properties is strictly prohibited. Plus, your new £1 home must be your main residence for at least five years. Notably, if you do live in the home for 10 years, then you'll find yourself in the very freeing and zen-like position of being rent and mortgage free.

If you buy a £1 home, you will be offered a loan of £30,000 to make the house habitable. At last, all those years as a nation being dripfed Sarah Beeny have come to fruition. These £1 homes are for people who do not fear the clatter of the wallpapering table and the slap of emulsion. Or at least don't mind making a lot of tea while a local painter and decorator does it. If you take out the loan, they want it back within 10 years – at an interest rate of 3 per cent above the Bank of England base rate, which is 0.5 per cent. Despite the strict rules, 600 people had applied for the homes within 24 hours. When something like the £1 house scheme seems as wholly reasonable and ethically watertight as this, I always try

to envisage who could possibly be offended or alienated. This is what halts progress at a local level. I watched, with some fascination, a local Lib Dem councillor spend many years opposing the regeneration of a dilapidated building for flats due to his "concerns about parking". There have been mumblings about the £1 houses, with claims that they are "patronising" and will only introduce ghettos. I've thought about this, and if it's a ghetto of people who really love DIY and faffing about with soft furnishings, I should like to buy a home very near to it.

Others suggest they should give all empty homes to a co-op, which fixes them up for people with no desire to "get on the property ladder". But, I'll whisper this, owning one's own home, and answering to no landlord, is a wholly agreeable state. Bulldozing broken communities, then telling the £25k earning bracket they wouldn't have wanted a £1 house anyway – now that sounds pretty damn patronising.

© *The Independent, 24 April 2013*
www.independent.co.uk

I've thought about this, and if it's a ghetto of people who really love DIY and faffing about with soft furnishings, I should like to buy a home very near to it.

Long-term renting is 'damaging children's lives'

EMILY DUGAN

One in 10 renting families have had to change their children's school in the past five years because they had to move home

SOME ISSUES:

Why do you think living in a rented house might affect somebody's life?

Why might moving house affect your school work or personal life?

How can more people be helped to buy homes?

Selected from Complete Issues:
Generation rent
Fact File 2012 p22
(see also Fact File 2014 for statistics on trends in home ownership)

Children's lives are being damaged by living in rented property, research says, as families across the country are being uprooted or left homeless by escalating rental costs.

One in five families now rent privately but many contracts are for only six or 12 months, leaving them at the mercy of landlords who can raise rents and turf out those who cannot afford new rates.

The problem is so acute that one in 10 renting families have had to change their children's school in the past five years because they had to move home.

Renting families are nine times more likely to have moved in the past year than those who own their homes. Parents are all too aware of the impact of this instability, with 44 per cent saying their child would have a better childhood if their home was more stable.

The figures are taken from the experiences of 4,000 English families renting property who were tracked by the homeless charity, Shelter, in the largest study of its kind. It found they were bearing the brunt of insecure tenancies, high rents and constant moves.

Antonia Bance, head of campaigns at Shelter, said: "Renting used to be a lifestyle choice but for many families now it's the only option they have. We've had this massive social change creep up on us without anyone really noticing the effect it has on children's lives and families."

Rents rose in 83 per cent of the country last year, but salaries stagnated, forcing many families to move in search of cheaper homes.

Labour has proposed a reform to privately rented housing, with longer-term tenancies and predictable rents. Jack Dromey MP, shadow housing minister, said: "Living a life of insecurity harms family life and blights the childhood of young people uprooted time and again from their schools and friends. Families must be able to plan where they send their kids to school and how they manage their household budgets."

A Department for Communities and Local Government spokesman

> **"Renting used to be a lifestyle choice but for many families now it's the only option they have. We've had this massive social change creep up on us without anyone really noticing the effect it has on children's lives and families."**

said: "There is no legal barrier to long-term tenancies. However, restrictive laws making this compulsory would mean fewer homes to rent, less choice and higher rents."

Almost four-fifths (79 per cent) of families who rent have an income of less than £40,000, compared with 58 per cent of the total population. Six in 10 cannot afford to buy a home.

© *The Independent*, 1 May 2013
www.independent.co.uk

Rents rose in 83 per cent of the country last year, but salaries stagnated, forcing many families to move in search of cheaper homes.

Case study: "I had a nervous breakdown because of all the moving"

Susan Sangster, 42, lives in Bedford with her sons Luke, 11, and Jake-Duke, three

"I've had to move eight times in the past seven years. Usually it was because the landlord put the rent up. Once we were evicted and the court hearing was on the day I gave birth to my youngest son. We had to spend six weeks in a homeless shelter that was full of cockroaches.

"I used to work part-time in catering but last year I had a nervous breakdown which was partly because of all the moving. Now I'm looking for work again. We moved to Bedford from West London in February because I just couldn't afford the rent and it seemed there was no-one to help. Now we're 80 miles away and we still haven't found somewhere for Luke to go to school. He left all his best friends behind and his teachers said it was a bad time for him to go, but I couldn't afford to stay."

The rich tax avoiders are the morally bankrupt ones

We're sick of people who don't want to play by the rules, who are only in it for themselves and don't give two hoots about the rest of us

Alison Phillips

Life's pretty lovely for actress Amanda Abbington. She's just starred in ITV's Mr Selfridge, she lives in a £900,000 house in leafy Hertfordshire and has two young children with her actor partner Martin Freeman.

Oh, and Martin is thought to be worth around £10million after his leading roles in movie blockbusters such as The Hobbit and Nativity. I'm guessing this isn't a family that is saving up their money-off coupons for Tesco right now.

So how come Amanda has just been pretty much let off a £120,000 tax bill by declaring herself bankrupt [*someone who is bankrupt is declared in law as unable to pay their debts*]? It is an absolute disgrace.

Most of us don't have any choice about whether we pay our tax or not. It's taken out of our pay packets before we even see it. And as a result we're all pitching in for hospitals, for schools and for policing.

But not Ms Abbington. She doesn't fancy shelling out for her local hospital and for police officers to walk the beat round her area. And presumably because she and her multi-millionaire partner can afford a fancy accountant, she doesn't have to either, because he's found her a way out of it.

As for the downsides of declaring herself bankrupt – not being able to manage her own finances and no access to credit – they're hardly a problem when your fella has just played the lead in a $1billion grossing film. With two more instalments still to come!

Fair? No, not remotely.

The right-wing papers feed us an endless diet of "benefits cheats" stories and, yes, it is easy to get riled about the old scrubbers with 11 kids who've never done a day's work in their lives. But the reality is that these people are few and far between.

In May 2011 just 8% of people claiming one out-of-work benefit had four or more children. That's 8% too many, some might argue. But the country isn't "overrun with scroungers". These aren't the biggest threat to the public purse – that comes from all those people who are avoiding paying their dues.

In recent months we've had Amazon, Starbucks and Google unwilling to pay their fair share in corporation tax. Now we've got the likes of Amanda Abbington refusing to pay her tax bill because she'd really rather not. Amanda has been with Martin for 10 years and they have two kids – even if she really is skint why on earth can't he chip in and help out with the bill?

In my house, like yours, we have our own money and a joint account too. But if there was a question of me going bankrupt I like to think

SOME ISSUES:

Do you think a person's partner should always support them financially?

In the UK in 2013 the basic rate of tax was 20%, higher rate was 40% and the highest rate was 45%. What percentage tax do you think people who earn most money should pay?

And what about people with far lower incomes?

Selected from Complete Issues:
Time to stop glossing over these artful tax dodgers
Essential Articles 14 p92
The hypocrisy of the filthy rich
Essential Articles 15 p78

Photo: Featureflash / Shutterstock.com

In recent months we've had Amazon, Starbucks and Google unwilling to pay their fair share in corporation tax.

my husband would step in and blow the moths from his wallet. But in the homes of the super-rich, relationships don't seem to work like that.

Topshop owner Sir Philip Green has avoided paying millions in tax by registering businesses in the name of his wife, who conveniently lives in Monaco. Meanwhile, we've had a host of other tax avoiders like Jimmy Carr, who have treated their tax bills as optional. And at the weekend we had millionaire film star Ray Winstone whingeing that he could imagine himself leaving Britain because he was sick of being "raped" by high taxes.

Fine, well, clear off Ray, because Britain will survive without you. And take Amanda Abbington, Bilbo Baggins and the woman with 11 kids with you too. Because we're sick of people who don't want to play by the rules – who are only in it for themselves and don't give two hoots about the rest of us. No one enjoys paying tax.

And right now there are millions and millions of people in real financial need who could really do with holding on to every penny that they possibly can. But they are paying their fair share. Those with the wealth to do the same but choose not to should hang their heads in shame

The Mirror, 13 March 2013

Right now there are millions and millions of people in real financial need who could really do with holding on to every penny that they possibly can. But they are paying their fair share. Those with the wealth to do the same but choose not to should hang their heads in shame.

i Editor's Letter:

What irritates me about bankers

Stefano Hatfield

We know, they know, they are horribly overpaid for whatever it is they do; and that it is hugely over-rated.

Have I mentioned one of the things that irritates me (and you) most about bankers? Their response to the dread "what do you do?" question is always a dismissive "I work in the City".

That's enough, see. That's all us "plebs" who do not work in the City need know. Not what they actually do, because so few of them can ever articulate that without resorting to an embarrassed self-deprecation that my friends who work in epidemiology, film, law, even advertising and journalism, don't feel the need for.

We know, they know, they are horribly overpaid for whatever it is they do; and that it is hugely over-rated. Money, as it is wont to do, blinded us to the nonsense of the destructively over-complicated financial tools they played with; mechanisms for making and losing vast sums that they themselves did not fully understand: gambling masquerading as banking.

It was worth it for them, because of that end-of-year bonus. Its justification to the outside world was always that banks needed to pay such astonishing sums to hire and retain the "very best talent".

Incredibly, this line is still trotted out, regardless that the "very best talent" got us all into this fine mess, because their corporate and personal greed was allowed to go largely unchecked. In what other walk of life could anyone argue that a bonus cap equivalent to one year's salary* (in addition to that salary) was not enough?

Although vested interests, and the lame "need to compete internationally" line may scupper the plan, it is difficult to see how anything other than that same greed can be used to justify rejecting this unusually sensible EU idea.

© The Independent, January 2013
www.independent.co.uk

*The EU has decided that bonuses for bank staff who earn €500,000 (£420,000) or more a year should be capped at 100% of their salary – or at 200% if shareholders give their approval

SOME ISSUES:

Does better pay automatically result in better results?

Is a limit on pay fair?

Which jobs deserve higher pay and which deserve lower?

Food &
drink

A young Briton with a lot on his plate - to stop the world wasting food Geoffrey Lean

A gala dinner in Kenya will highlight the millons of tons of food wasted all over the world. All the food on the menu will have been thrown away

THE GALA DINNER: On Tuesday 19th February 2013 a five-course meal made from waste African fruit and vegetables was served to 500 delegates at a United Nations Environment Programme (UNEP) event in Nairobi, Kenya.

The food would all have fallen below the standards required by European buyers for European supermarkets and would otherwise have been left to rot or at best fed to livestock. Buyers for supermarkets in Europe will reject fruit and vegetables purely because they are not the perfect shape, size or colour.

The banquet was intended to highlight how perfectly edible food is being wasted. It included grilled sweet corn tamales, yellow lentil dhal and a tropical version of the Italian dessert tiramisu, called mangomisu.

In 10 days' time, 500 ministers, top bureaucrats, UN officials, pressure group leaders and associated hangers-on will sit down to a banquet in Nairobi. Nothing unusual about that, you may say. It's par for the course at international conferences, the sort of thing that gets some on the Right grumbling about waste, and some on the Left mumbling about taking food from the mouths of the poor.

But this one will be different. Every scrap served at the gala dinner at the Global Ministerial Environment Forum in the Kenyan capital will have been thrown away, part of the mountain range of edible food that goes to waste worldwide. And it will mark the moment that a campaign to reduce it, started by a young Briton, goes global.

The extent of the waste, which will be starkly set out in statistics on the diners' napkins, is shaming. The United Nations Environment Programme (UNEP), which is hosting the meeting, and the Food and Agriculture Organisation (FAO) conservatively estimate that a third of all the food produced worldwide each year – worth more than $1 trillion – is never eaten. And this when hundreds of millions already cannot get enough and the world's population is expected to swell by another two billion in less than three decades.

The waste also uses up other scarce resources. Some 500 million hectares of arable land – an area larger than the Indian subcontinent – grows unconsumed food. So forests are cut down and vital wetlands drained to provide land that should not be used. And there is also a massive waste of water, energy and fertiliser.

Yet buried in the scandal lies an opportunity. Cutting food waste by just a quarter, as the delegates' napkins will remind them, would release enough – in

SOME ISSUES:

Why is food waste a problem?

Does your family waste food?

What could you do to reduce this?

Britain is one of the most wasteful countries: the average family discards food worth £480 a year.

theory – to feed all the world's 870 million desperately hungry people. Destruction of wild places could be greatly reduced, the release of greenhouse gases curbed and water conserved.

That would demand changes in rich and poor countries alike. In developed nations, most waste occurs because producers, retailers and consumers throw out food that is still fit for consumption. A third of what is grown never reaches the market – largely because it fails to meet cosmetic standards demanded by supermarkets – while consumers throw out 222 million tons of food a year, almost as much as sub-Saharan Africa produces.

Britain is one of the most wasteful countries: the average family discards food worth £480 a year. One way or another, by some calculations, up to two thirds of the vegetables grown in Britain go uneaten.

Of course, cutting back on waste in rich countries does not mean that the liberated food ends up in the stomachs of the poor in developing ones. But by reducing demand, it can bring down prices, enabling needy people to buy more.

In developing countries, 95 per cent of the waste occurs before the food is sold, eaten by pests on the farm or rotting in markets, through poor storage and distribution. In India, 21 million tons of wheat –

equivalent to Australia's entire production – perishes in this way annually, while enough food is lost in Africa to feed 300 million people.

Now, at last, the world is beginning to address the issue. Much of this is down to Tristram Stuart, who, when feeding pigs at 15, realised how much good food went into their troughs. Over the last two decades he has studied the issues, examined bins behind supermarkets, written a book and organised a feeding of 5,000 people on waste food in Trafalgar Square in 2009. He is also behind the Nairobi dinner, which will help launch a global campaign by UNEP and the FAO. And already things are happening. Partly inspired by Stuart, Britain has been a pioneer, with successive governments launching anti-waste pushes. Waste in homes fell by 17 per cent between 2007 and 2010, he says, while sales of odd-shaped fruit and veg rose by 300,000 tons last year.

France has also initiated a campaign. South Korea has introduced swipe-card bins, charging households for food they throw out. And in China, the presumptive new president, Xi Jinping, has cracked down on banquets and launched a "Clear the Plate" drive, decreeing: "These habits of waste must be stopped immediately!"

"I don't know exactly how it works," says Stuart, "but it does. People are amazed – and shocked – by the problem, and want to help. It is a relief in many ways that we can enhance the lives of the world's hungry and reduce pressure on land by doing things as easy as buying only the food we eat, and eating whatever we buy."

Daily Telegraph, 8 February 2013
© Telegraph Media Group Limited 2013

Fairtrade, ethical eating, and why the choice between buying local and global is a distraction

What does good food actually mean?

JULIAN BAGGINI

Spot the contradiction. Today, a conscientious, ethical consumer might celebrate the start of Fairtrade Fortnight by walking into a local, independent grocery store in the Southwest of England and filling his basket with honey, herbs, chocolate, dried apricots, bananas, even wine from the developing world. He might then go to the till, walking past innumerable signs boasting of how much of the shop's stock is sourced locally, and pay in a local currency, the Bristol Pound*, which uses the slogan "Our city. Our money".

Injustice

To say there is a tension here is to put it mildly. Yet both Fairtrade and the new localism can be reconciled as two parts of the solution to the same problem: the injustice and unfairness of the current market economy.

Take Fairtrade first. It addresses the problems caused by what Harriet Lamb, chief executive of Fairtrade International, calls the "hourglass economy". With coffee, for example, about 25 million smallholders worldwide produce 80 per cent of the world's coffee, which ends up being drunk by millions of consumers.

But between producer and consumer are just a handful of middlemen, often using their market dominance to squeeze producers. Forty per cent of the global coffee market is in the hands of four companies, and 60 per cent of the retail trade is captured by five global brands.

SOME ISSUES:

Why is Fairtrade a good thing?

Why should people buy their food from local producers?

What are the negative effects of buying local?

Which do you think is the fairest way to buy?

Why should money in one of the wealthier areas of the world remain there, rather than go to those who need it more?

Photo: Thomas Demol

Fairtrade restores an equitable link between producer groups – usually working together in co-operatives – and consumers, reducing the proportion creamed off by third parties. It gives producers in the developing world a better deal, until world trade rules are reformed to make such individual efforts unnecessary.

Buying local can be another way to promote equitable relationships between consumers, retailers and producers. As the Bristol Pound campaign puts it, "With sterling, much of the wealth spent in the city is lost to big international business, related management structures, remote shareholders and the boom-bust of the financial banking system".

Who is most deserving?

So the key issue is not whether money stays locally or moves internationally, it's that a fair share of it goes to the farmers, workers and producers who make the things we trade. Advocates of localism often ignore or miss this point. The Bristol Pound campaign, for example, boasts that it "helps wealth created in Bristol to stay here."

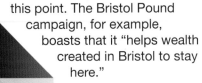

But why should money in one of the wealthier areas of the world remain there, rather than go to those who need it more?

Fairtrade Fortnight should serve as a reminder that resisting the most egregious excesses of the market economy does not require a choice between trading locally or globally. We should support good, local independent businesses but we also need what Carlos Petrini, the founder of Slow Food, calls "virtuous globalisation".

Progressives need to retain and refresh their internationalist aspirations so that the ethos of "go local" does not become a selfish parochial dogma.

© The Independent, 24 February 2013
www.independent.co.uk

*The Bristol Pound is money which has the same value as the UK pound but can only be spent at Bristol businesses. The idea is to keep money within the city so that small, independent, local businesses can thrive.

Paltrow's recipe for eating disorders

Grace Dent

Being a woman is very often hard. You may have heard me occasionally mention it. Thank heavens we've got Gwyneth Paltrow's new quack-science, semi-starvation recipe book, It's All Good, being shoved down our throats on every TV show to keep us zinging with energy.

Paltrow is a lovely, watchable actress. She has a likeable sense of humour in interviews. I like her husband Chris. I am not anti-Gwyneth. However, I am against the wholly cynical, harmful machine-pushing of a famous woman – who has endless Hollywood-style food allergies and phobias, and who arguably needs to fit into size zero costumes to earn her living – into the role of food expert. I am not alluding to the idea that Paltrow barely eats; that's there as fact in full colour with hundreds of feeble dinner-dodging words.

> Back in the real world, if I saw a young girl with that on her plate, I'd think: "That's an eating disorder."

Doctors – of whom she has seen many – have decreed Paltrow to be allergic to pretty much everything, including peppers, corn and aubergine. The book's recipes are designed to facilitate a short-term elimination diet that eschews processed foods, coffee, alcohol, dairy, eggs, sugar, shellfish, deep-water fish, wheat, meat, and soy. Sometimes she lets loose and has pomegranate and quinoa. Behold the dinner suggestion – featured on last week's Goop newsletter – of a small poached egg, three grilled spring onions and two small steamed pieces of broccoli. Two hundred calories of pure sustenance. Yummy.

Back in the real world, if I was queuing up in the office canteen and saw a young girl with that on her plate, I'd think: "That's an eating disorder. I hope she's got someone keeping an eye on her." But with an Oscar and an Emmy under her belt, suddenly we're asking her for weight-loss tips. Life is short: get some macaroni cheese and a glass of red down your throat. I can assure you, it won't kill you.

© The Independent, 24 April 2013
www.independent.co.uk

SOME ISSUES:

Do you think celebrities are good role models when it comes to food and diet?

What pressures might actors and models be under regarding what they eat and their appearance?

Whose advice about food and diets would you listen to?

See also:
Complete Issues
Body image and Eating disorders

Photo: DFree Shutterstock.com

FLEXITARIANISM: FOR VEGGIES WHO JUST CAN'T RESIST A BACON BUTTY

'Flexible vegetarianism' is on the rise

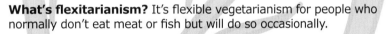

What's flexitarianism? It's flexible vegetarianism for people who normally don't eat meat or fish but will do so occasionally.

Not really vegetarian at all then? They are often referred to as vegivores. Unlike the rest of us, meat doesn't dominate their diet but it isn't completely ruled out as with true vegetarians.

So basically they're cheating? Maybe better to think of them as part-time veggies.

And why are we talking about them? Because according to a survey we are likely to be joining them. The Food People who carried out the survey expect "meat-free eating and flexitarianism soon to be a mega trend." They predict a "notable increase in flexitarian – or demi-vegetarian – eating" in Britain.

Why? Well cutting down on meat makes eating cheaper. The vegetarian option is said to be healthier too but many people can't manage to go completely veggie. Then there's the ethical argument and the horse meat scandal, I could go on...

Please don't. Just tell me who's behind this idea The McCartneys, of course. The survey was commissioned by Linda McCartney Foods, the meat-free company founded by Sir Paul's late wife. Sir Paul and his daughters also launched the meat-free Mondays campaign to encourage us to eat veggie once a week.

Who else supports it? Gwyneth Paltrow, Sir Richard Branson, Cameron Diaz and Joss Stone.

But they can all afford to eat steak and caviar for every meal! Even if they do eat meat they try to make sure it is from an ethical source and environmentally friendly, so as well as being flexitarians they are ecotarians.

Say what? Ecotarians only eat foods that have the least impact on the environment.

So Richard Branson will eat a chicken leg but only if it comes from a bird that's lived a happy life and never clocked up any air miles on his planes? You may mock but flexitarianism can be a gateway into the harder stuff, vegetarianism or veganism (no meat, milk, eggs or anything that uses animals in its production).

If the meat's free on Mondays I'll have a bacon butty!

Sources: various

SOME ISSUES:

Do you think flexitarianism is a cop-out compared to being a vegetarian?

Why is it important to eat less meat?

What other benefits might flexitarianism have?

WILLY WONKA'S FRUIT AND VEG FACTORY

Photo: Thomas Demol

SOME ISSUES:

Do we really need new foods?

What would make a great new food?

Should all our efforts go into growing more food not new varieties?

(see also Fact File 2014 for figures on eating well)

Don't want to eat your greens?

Struggling to come to terms with your five-a-day?

There are people working for years to make fruit and veg ever more appetising, or at least different.

Each year the international trade fair Fruit Logistica sees growers competing to wow the buyers of the big supermarkets so that they, in turn, can wow their customers. The result is an array of colours and flavours to rival Willy Wonka's sweet factory.

In 2013 a British firm, Tozer Seeds, won third place for outstanding innovation at Fruit Logistica with a brand new vegetable: the Flower Sprout. A cross between two 'Superfoods', Brussels sprouts and kale, it is the size of a sprout but prettier, looking like a tiny cabbage with green frilly leaves streaked with purple.

This new vegetable has the looks and the health credentials (extra vitamin B6 and vitamin C) to be a success. Crucially, though, Flower Sprouts have a mild, sweet 'nutty' flavour. Top retailers are stocking them in the hope of converting their sprout-resistant customers.

Around the world, plant breeders are experimenting with the flavour and size of our fruit and veg. You can buy plums that smell and taste like bubblegum, tiny kiwi fruit the size of a grape and grapes that taste like mangoes. Black Velvet is the enticing name of a plum/apricot hybrid – plum size with a velvety fuzz and with the yellow flesh of an apricot. Carrots now come in pale cream or purple. Mayan Twilight potatoes have striped purple skins.

We are talking here of traditional breeding methods not the so-called 'Frankenstein foods' produced by genetic modification. Still, improving on nature strikes some customers as actually unnatural and they resist new varieties. But 'improved' breeding is hardly new. The orange carrot we know now was developed by the Dutch in the 17th century as part of their struggle for independence and their support of William of Orange, before that carrots came in varieties of purple, white, red, yellow and even black.

Perhaps the correct comparison for the new fruit and veg is not "Charlie and the Chocolate Factory" but "Back to the Future".

Source: Various

Photo: Tozer Seeds

Gender

Not just a girl...

Let's show our girls the REAL women they can be

"Now and then women should do for themselves what men have already done - occasionally what men have not done - thereby establishing themselves as persons, and perhaps encouraging other women toward greater independence of thought and action."

Amelia Earheart

Jaime Moore

So my amazing daughter, Emma, turned 5 last month, and I had been searching everywhere for new-creative inspiration for her 5 year pictures. I noticed quite a pattern of so many young girls dressing up as beautiful Disney Princesses, no matter where I looked 95% of the "ideas" were the "How tos" of how to dress your little girl like a Disney Princess. Now don't get me wrong, I LOVE Disney Princesses, from their beautiful dresses, perfect hair, gorgeous voices and most with ideal love stories in the mix you can't help but become entranced with the characters. But it got me thinking, they're just characters, a writer's tale of a princess (most before 1998)... an unrealistic fantasy for most girls (Yay Kate Middleton!).

It started me thinking about all the REAL women for my daughter to know about and look up to, REAL women who without ever meeting Emma have changed her life for the better. My daughter wasn't born into royalty, but she was born into a country where she can now vote, become a doctor, a pilot, an astronaut, or even President if she wants and that's what REALLY matters. I wanted her to know the value of these amazing women who had gone against everything so she can now have everything. We chose 5 women (5 amazing and strong women), as it was her 5th birthday but there are thousands of unbelievable women (and girls) who have beaten the odds and fought (and still fight) for their equal rights all over the world... so let's set aside the Barbie Dolls and the Disney Princesses for just a moment, and let's show our girls the REAL women they can be.

SOME ISSUES:

Do you think Disney Princesses are positive or negative role models?

Who do you think is a positive role model for young men and women?

What do you know about the 5 women chosen as role models? The other two, not illustrated here, are Jane Goodall and Susan R Anthony

Gender

Dear Graham: My son wants to quit football for dancing - his dad isn't happy

Agony uncle, Graham Norton, answers readers' personal problems

SOME ISSUES:

Why do you think the boy's father is embarrassed about his interest in dancing?

Does this seem unreasonable to you?

What do you think Mrs K should do?

Selected from Complete Issues:
My 14 year old son is displaying very strong homosexual tendencies
Essential Articles 15 p64

Dear Graham,

My husband, a keen amateur footballer, runs a club for the kids around here. He's proud of his teams and the fact that our 14-year-old son plays for one of them. At first our boy quite liked playing and making friends with the other boys but I could see from the start that football wasn't really his thing. He's a keen musician and, much to his father's embarrassment, loves dancing. He's got a friend – male – who does ballet and modern dance and last weekend, as I drove him back from this friend's house, he asked me if it is wrong that he wants to give dance lessons a go too. I told him that it's not exactly wrong, but that his father would have a fit if he got wind of it.

Just as I thought, my husband was very angry when I gently mentioned it to him and said he was going to have some "strong words" with our boy that evening. I didn't hear the conversation but my son is continuing to play football and my husband thinks the situation is resolved. It's not, though. My son has asked me if I'll pay for dance lessons. I'm not keen, particularly as it undermines my husband, but I also don't want to make my son unhappy.

Mrs K, Dorset

"He's a keen musician and, much to his father's embarrassment, loves dancing"

"Your son has asked to try out dancing, not heroin"

Dear Mrs K,

I'm not a parent but I like to think I'd be a little less blinkered than your husband. Your son has asked to try out dancing, not heroin. As the voice of reason, I fear you will have to be the go-between. Your son isn't saying he wants to quit football altogether, so get his dad to tell you why the idea of dancing is so terrible. Does he think it will lead to bullying? Is he worried your son is gay or does it somehow reflect badly on his own masculinity? None of these seem like very valid excuses. As a 14-year-old in school, your son will know more about bullying than you or your husband and he is willing to take the risk. When it comes to masculinity and sexuality, it seems crazy to build them into huge issues that will in turn become enormous barriers between you all.

Your husband may have had a dream scenario in his head where his boy became Roy of the Rovers, but it strikes me that if he takes a step back, he should be enormously proud of a son who has passions and the strength of character to try something new.

Up until now, you have had a man and a boy in the house and it is only natural that as the boy becomes a man in his own right, there will be conflict. Don't let this situation spiral out of control with secrets and sides. Be open and honest. Your husband isn't going to get the perfect mini-me, so stop looking for someone who isn't there and start seeing the young man you have raised.

If you want something to grow, it's always best to encourage it, not step on it with a heavy boot. If all else fails, sit them both down in front of a DVD of Billy Elliot. Good luck.

Graham Norton

The Daily Telegraph, 5 November 2012
© *Telegraph Media Group Limited 2012*

We need more men to fight sexism

CATRIONA STEWART

LUNCH recently with friends and the subject of heckling comes up...

Heckling, groping, harassment. Every one of us has a story to tell. Every one. And not just anecdotes about the odd catcall in the street or tea-making jibes in the office.

Here's one of mine: on the train home from my first visit to Manchester a man sat down next to me, and undid his tracksuit bottoms. There were only three other people in the carriage at the time, one another young woman, who was really quite shaken. He'd been sporadically bothering both of us before the grand finale and she hadn't known what to do. My new friend was about 6ft 4in with his tracksuit trousers tucked into Homer Simpson socks. I gave him what my grandmother liked to call a Paddington stare and excused myself. The ticket collector, when I asked him to, refused to call the police. When I told my tutor at uni she said: "I hate when that happens."

That's an extreme example but harassment in myriad forms is par for the course for women. This week this issue made UK-wide headlines when Glasgow University Union (GUU) became the backdrop for a shameful debating chamber debacle as two of the top-rated student debaters in the world were harangued by sexist chants from their male peers. A female judge was called a "frigid b***h" when she complained.

SOME ISSUES:

Why do you think heckling is a bad thing?

Do you see this type of behaviour occurring around you?

What can women do to tackle this?

What can men do to help the issue?

Why should men also tackle sexism?

They think it's complimentary rather than insulting, objectifying and, at times, intimidating.

A website where women can record their experiences of being harassed in public or at work has received more than 20,000 entries.

My friend Nadine says she'd like to do some kind of feminist ninja training. When you're on the receiving end of slithering tentacles or sleazy words it's difficult not to want to deliver a hard fist to soft regions. I like the thought of a band of renegade feminist ninjas roaming the streets, twisting the fingers of groping hands and pinching catcalling tongues.

This topic was touched on this week by my colleague Alan Taylor*. He says we need more difficult women. We do. We also need more men, like Alan, who are willing to recognise it. It's tricky for men, I think, to get it right sometimes. The smart ones will worry about seeming paternalistic.

My favourite entry so far on ESP is from a woman who says: "Dear random man who lifted his top up when builders shouted 'get yer t*** out' at me, thanks. You made my day." I like the thought of feminist ninjas. I like the thought better of more men like this one, taking sides. That's not paternalism, it's teamwork. And that's what we need.

Herald Scotland, 9 March 2013

Alan Taylor wrote about the American writer Lilian Hellman "She did not suffer fools at all and gave short shrift to anyone she thought merited it. We could do with a few more like her around nowadays". He concluded "if women want to have equality they're going to have to fight tooth and nail to get it. For no-one is going to help them"

Harassment in myriad forms is par for the course for women.

This is a red rag to a bullish feminist. It is disgusting. But not surprising.

Journalist Laura Bates last year set up the Everyday Sexism Project (ESP), a website where women can record their experiences of being harassed in public or at work and it's received more than 20,000 entries. On Tuesday a Glasgow page was set up, the GUU Everyday Sexism Project, on Facebook, and it too is heavy with entries.

I wrote previously about Hollaback, a website similar to the Everyday Sexism Project, set up in 2011 also to record street harassment. A lovely old gentleman wrote in with the very best of intentions to tell me that my problem is I'm just "too bonny". For street harassment apologists this is the issue: they think it's complimentary rather than insulting, objectifying and, at times, intimidating.

I like the thought of feminist ninjas roaming the street, twisting the fingers of groping hands

A burgeoning men's rights movement in British universities? Lads, you cannot be serious

Even if you've already heard from the online 'masculism' mob, the men's rights comments under a recent Independent article must be read to be believed

TOM MENDELSOHN

It is official: men are an oppressed minority these days. Despite an entire human history's-worth of cultural dominance, in the few short generations since women got the vote, feminism has spoiled it for everyone, and women have full, unnatural dominance.

You don't believe me? Consider this: who dies more often in wars, men or women? Which sex has the shorter life expectancy? Who has to make all the alimony payments? And who, most of all, has to leave a sinking cruise ship in last place? If you answered 'men' (poor, browbeaten men) to all of these, you'd be right, though these examples only scratch the surface of the systemic inequities men are forced to face each and every day.

There's the pressure of having to pay for the bill on a date, more often than not, and that of having to conform to that terrible Hollywood stereotype of having, like, big pectoral muscles and things. Feminism has inculcated a crisis in masculinity.

Well that's what I would say, if I had, as the ghastly Men's Rights movement puts it with the full cod-philosophical force of the Matrix movies, swallowed 'the red pill'.

Men's Rights is a movement that, while not exclusive to the internet, has blossomed – or festered, however you prefer it to put it – online. It's

Men's Rights is loopy. Men aren't oppressed. We've had a pretty good thing going since the year dot, since that one time Eve was conjured as a divine afterthought from Adam's spare rib.

loopy. Of course it's loopy. Men aren't oppressed. We've had a pretty good thing going since the year dot, since that one time Eve was conjured as a divine afterthought from Adam's spare rib. Feminism, as a movement, is nothing more than an attempt to recalibrate society into something that doesn't completely overwhelm men with favour. And however well you might think it has succeeded, it really hasn't, what with glass ceilings, pats on bottoms and the endless bloody trumpetings of the whooping online 'masculism' mob.

Allow me, as The Independent's online student editor, to mention an article, in which we documented the struggle of a few young women brave enough to try and establish a feminist society at York. York's Student Union won't ratify them for what may look to the untrained eye as spurious reasons, most of which boil down to 'it's unnecessary'.

As if to demonstrate how unnecessary such a society may be, the article has attracted 300 brave comments below the line, each painstakingly typed one-fingered.

'SANDWICH!!!' concludes one sage, a persuasive argument underlined through nifty deployment of exclamation points. Beneath him, ha ha, one sweetalkinguy makes a subtle point of his own: 'Hysteria!' – like what women get when they're worked up, his brief remark a beacon of reason in a dark world of appeals to woolly girl-thought.

It isn't just men who are so angry about the damage that feminism hath wrought on the 21st Century. Thoughtful Kelly Jessop believes, in all apparent seriousness, that 'feminism is a hate movement' which causes 'men to take their lives'.

Then there are the people who attempt to inject class and race into the issue, as though the white British working man is somehow the most put-upon male constituency of all. This thinking is never fully explained, but it's possibly something to do with, I suppose, how easy urban black youths have it these days.

I'm sure a lot of these ornery young dudes are complaining like this for a reason: they're constantly reminded of what a privilege it is for them to be men, but don't feel, as students in modern Coalition Britain, all the many benefits of this privilege. And yes, there are genuine issues faced by men, even body image ones. But what our commenters might not be getting, with their angry desire for egalitarianism above feminism, is that feminism fights their cause too.

The rad fem man-haters are dying off these days, and the hip feminists aren't trying to #killallmen so much as smash the patriarchy. A patriarchy, that is, that harms men as well as women, with its promotion of masculinity and men as stoic providers, and femininity with women as an underclass of nurturers.

But to the people calling for 'masculism' or 'safe spaces for men', who see 'misandry' every time a woman wants a platform to make demands, well, sirs, you are idiots. The masculinity you base these incessant demands for sandwiches, sluts and spurious recognition of temperamental differences between the sexes is not positive, helpful or remotely egalitarian.

And at least until we can run articles about campus feminist organisations without rolling in MRM ordure, the need for feminist organisations on our campuses will remain abundantly clear.

© The Independent, 9 May 2013
www.independent.co.uk

Feminism, as a movement, is nothing more than an attempt to recalibrate society into something that doesn't completely overwhelm men with favour.

Screenshot of Caroline Lucas speaking out about Page Three

EVERYDAY SEXISM starts on PAGE THREE and ends up in our lives

SOME ISSUES:

Do you think having 'Page Three Girls' in newspapers encourages sexism?

Why is sexism bad?

Does removing the 'Page Three Girl' affect freedom of speech?

What can be done to tackle sexist behaviour and sexual assault?

Selected from Complete Issues: Helen, 28, has some thoughts on Page Three *Essential Articles 15 p100*

See also:
It's time for girls to toughen up on sexual harassment... p106

NO MORE PAGE THREE

When The Sun newspaper started to feature topless models on its page 3 in November 1970 it immediately drew protests. Campaigners objected to the way women were simply used as decoration and titillation. In 2012 Lucy-Anne Holmes breathed new life into the protests by beginning the "No More Page Three" campaign and using social media to spread her message.

She began with an online petition which rapidly gathered support, then extended her campaign via Twitter to include street protests and flash mobs making a very visible objection to the presence of "Page Three girls" in newspapers.

She explains her motivation: "The Page Three girl image is there for no other reason than the sexual gratification of men. She's a sex object. But when figures range from 300,000 women being sexually assaulted and 60,000 raped each year, to 1 in 4 who have been sexually assaulted, is it wise to be repeatedly perpetuating a notion that women are sexual objects?"

Coalition leaders David Cameron and Nick Clegg both dismissed the issue as unimportant, responding with patronising statements like "just shut the paper" and "if you don't like it don't buy paper" and "if you don't like it don't buy it". Their view is not shared by Green MP Caroline Lucas who wore a 'No More Page Three' t-shirt at the start of a debate in the House of Commons about sexism in the media. She was asked to cover it up since MPs are not allowed to display slogans or debating points. Vigorously supporting the campaign, she said Page Three images were not acceptable in a family newspaper seen by up to 7.5m people each day.

Opponents of the campaign refer to freedom of speech but fail to acknowledge that whether as an individual you choose to buy newspapers like The Sun or not, the images are a part of the world that we live in; present on the newspaper stands we pass, in the cafes we where we drink. As Caroline Lucas says "Page Three is a symbol of this problem. It 'normalises' the idea that women are there primarily for men's sexual pleasure and, whilst I and other MPs can chose not to buy the paper, we are, nonetheless, through the choices of others... unable to avoid Page Three."

EVERYDAY SEXISM

Even before Holmes began her fight, another campaigning woman was also using social media to hit out at the sexism that most women encounter everyday creating the Everday Sexism Project

Laura Bates knew that many people do not feel comfortable speaking out about

Page Three is a symbol of this problem. It 'normalises' the idea that women are there primarily for men

experiences of sexism, or even actual sexual assault: victims wrongly feel embarrassed or somehow responsible. Sexism, particularly casual sexism that doesn't necessarily cause physical harm, is seen as a 'bit of fun.' It is so commonplace that many victims do not feel entitled to speak out against it.

But Bates offered a solution. As it says on the website: "The Everyday Sexism Project exists to catalogue sexism experienced

Sexism affects men as well as women. Children from as young as seven to adult women of over 70 have shared their experiences on the site, highlighting strongly that sexism is a very real problem.

by women on a day to day basis. They might be serious or minor, outrageously offensive or so niggling and normalised that you don't even feel able to protest."

People are encouraged to upload their experiences to the website or to tweet it to @everydaysexism. You can remain anonymous if you want to. This is a means of supporting victims and getting the word out that routine sexism is not an acceptable part of life.

Laura Bates wrote in 2012: "I never imagined that by now it would have attracted some 25,000 entries and be about to spread to 15 countries". Experiences are hugely wide-ranging and affect men as well as women. Children from as young as seven to adult women of over 70 have shared their experiences on the site, highlighting strongly that sexism is a very real problem.

These campaigns and their high profile support are encouraging more and more people to speak out. This issue cannot be ignored any longer. As Lucy Anne Holmes says: "People have had enough of a media that treats women as being primarily there for decoration and titillation... and seeks to silence those who speak up... with taunts of 'you're ugly and jealous'.

"It's quite simple really – we want to see women represented with respect in the media."

This will mean women are respected in society, which is exactly how it should be!

**For more information visit:
nomorepage3.org
@nomorepage3
www.everydaysexism.com
@everydaysexism**

Sources: Various

Excerpts from the everydaysexism website

Shanna via Twitter   2013-06-13 14:56
Why are women in the Apprentice boardroom 'girls' but men are never boys?

Caroline via Twitter   2013-06-13 14:53
Just got wolf-whistled at while scanning items at the supermarket. WTF. It's not a compliment, it's invasive.

Helen   2013-05-24 20:01
For years men on the street who are total strangers have asked me to "smile". These men would never ask a man on the street to smile. These men don't even know it's sexist.

Ha   2013-05-24 20:00
My brother got the toys I wanted, I got dolls. We swapped. My mum let us and she got criticised. Thank goodness my mum isn't an idiot.

Baba   2013-05-24 19.35
Bloke "admitted" to me he was a full time dad/househusband – I said that's nice, have you seen "comando dad" the website for househusbands? The relief on his face. Apparently he'd been getting stick about his life choice. A lot of men don't realise that feminism is very much in favour of men who choose this role.

Not just a girl...

Let's show our girls the REAL women they can be

"Now and then women should do for themselves what men have already done - occasionally what men have not done - thereby establishing themselves as persons, and perhaps encouraging other women toward greater independence of thought and action."

Amelia Earheart

Jaime Moore

SOME ISSUES:

Do you think Disney Princesses are positive or negative role models?

Who do you think is a positive role model for young men and women?

What do you know about the 5 women chosen as role models? The other two, not illustrated here, are Jane Goodall and Susan R Anthony

So my amazing daughter, Emma, turned 5 last month, and I had been searching everywhere for new-creative inspiration for her 5 year pictures. I noticed quite a pattern of so many young girls dressing up as beautiful Disney Princesses, no matter where I looked 95% of the "ideas" were the "How tos" of how to dress your little girl like a Disney Princess. Now don't get me wrong, I LOVE Disney Princesses, from their beautiful dresses, perfect hair, gorgeous voices and most with ideal love stories in the mix you can't help but become entranced with the characters. But it got me thinking, they're just characters, a writer's tale of a princess (most before 1998)... an unrealistic fantasy for most girls (Yay Kate Middleton!).

It started me thinking about all the REAL women for my daughter to know about and look up to, REAL women who without ever meeting Emma have changed her life for the better. My daughter wasn't born into royalty, but she was born into a country where she can now vote, become a doctor, a pilot, an astronaut, or even President if she wants and that's what REALLY matters. I wanted her to know the value of these amazing women who had gone against everything so she can now have everything. We chose 5 women (5 amazing and strong women), as it was her 5th birthday but there are thousands of unbelievable women (and girls) who have beaten the odds and fought (and still fight) for their equal rights all over the world... so let's set aside the Barbie Dolls and the Disney Princesses for just a moment, and let's show our girls the REAL women they can be.

"Be of good cheer. Do not think of today's failures, but of the success that may come tomorrow. You have set yourselves a difficult task, but you will succeed if you persevere. What I am looking for is not out there, it is in me." Helen Keller

It started me thinking about all the REAL women for my daughter to know about and look up to, REAL women who without ever meeting Emma have changed her life for the better.

"In order to be irreplaceable one must always be different – Life isn't about finding yourself, it's about creating yourself – A girl should be two things: who and what she wants." Coco Chanel

I wanted her to know the value of these amazing women who had gone against everything so she can now have everything.

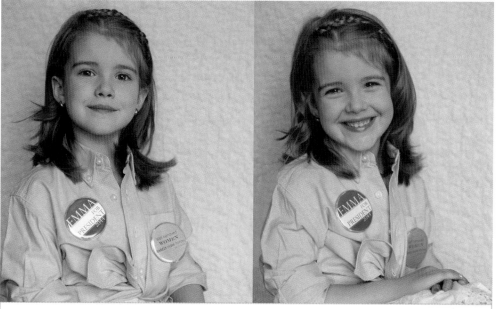

Let's show our girls the *Real* women they can be

Source: www.jaimemoorephotography.com

IT IS TIME FOR GIRLS TO 'TOUGHEN UP' ON SEXUAL HARASSMENT AND SCHOOLS MUST TEACH THEM HOW

RACHEL ROBERTS

SOME ISSUES:

Is this sort of sexist behaviour as common as the writer says?

How can young women tackle the issue?

How can young men tackle the issue?

See also:
Everyday sexism p108

On February 14th, people around the world gathered to mark the One Billion Rising campaign to end violence against women and girls. That same day, on a rather smaller scale, my niece celebrated her thirteenth birthday. Sadly – but perhaps not surprisingly – she had already encountered sexual harassment before she even became a teenager. Nothing terribly newsworthy, just the casual, low-level abuse experienced by women and girls on a daily basis – remarks about her appearance and name-calling by boys at school, being embarrassed in public by a charming young chap who asked her if she knew how to give a blow-job, being followed round a shop by a group of older boys discussing her anatomy and whether she was worth "doing" – all par for the course for a young girl growing up in Britain today.

In the news

Everything in the news at the moment suggests a 13-year-old girl had better get used to it, because from the Lord Rennard scandal *[Liberal Democrat accused by*

female colleagues of sexual molestation] to the thousands of stories catalogued by the Everyday Sexism Project *[Twitter project highlighting daily sexism]*, there are more tales of sexual harassment rearing their ugly heads than you can shake a stick at. My niece is one of the lucky ones. She is from a loving family, has a mother she can talk openly with and is a confident child who isn't afraid to stand up for herself. Not all children are so fortunate, which is why the role of the school is vital in teaching staff and pupils how to recognise and challenge sexual bullying.

Sexist bullying

The academy attended by my niece apparently has a robust anti-bullying policy, and her year eight group had one session on sexist bullying, which she found useful. But she told me: "I think the main thing they are bothered about (in sex education) is teaching us not to get pregnant while we're still at school…. a lot of the girls don't say anything when boys call them names or insult them because they don't really think it's bullying. They just laugh along with it, but it's not really funny." When I ask her what she thinks girls should do in these situations, she considers for a moment and replies: "They could tell a teacher – a good one, who'll take it seriously. But to be honest, I think some of the girls need to grow a pair and stick up for themselves more." Harsh words, perhaps, although in keeping with former Lib Dem spin doctor, Jo Phillips, who suggested last week that women in politics who feared sexual harassment might need to "toughen up" a bit.

Physical & sexual violence

I would never wish to blame the victim, and the statistics on the assault of young girls make depressing reading. A YouGov poll found nearly one in three 16-18 year-old girls had experienced groping or unwanted sexual touching at school, whilst an NSPCC survey revealed that nearly a third of girls aged 13-17 in a relationship had experienced physical or sexual violence. The Schools Safe 4 Girls campaign was launched by the End Violence Against Women coalition last year, calling on schools to help educate pupils in how to make more informed choices regarding sexual behaviour. But how can this be done, and how can girls (and sometimes boys) gain the confidence to speak out against sexual bullying?

Sex & relationship education

To coincide with the One Billion Rising campaign, the Commons debated and passed a motion calling on the Government to make sex and relationship education in all schools statutory. Currently, parents can exclude their children from Personal, Sexual, Health and Economics education (PSHE), and academies and free schools are not obliged to offer it at all, although many do. The motion was proposed following a campaign spearheaded by Labour's Stella Creasy, but whether a bill makes it onto the statute remains to be seen. The Government has proved reluctant to legislate for sex and relationship education in the past, and all of the Ministers for Education were notable only by their absence during the debate.

Prevention is always better than the cure, and the issue of how boys and girls relate to one another should be addressed as soon as children go to secondary school – well before most kids actually start having sex. Bringing in youth workers from outside the school could yield positive results,

BOTH SEXES SHOULD BE TAUGHT TO RECOGNISE EMOTIONAL ABUSE AND CONTROLLING BEHAVIOUR

since teachers may not be well trained in relationship and sex education. As the Conservative MP Dr Sarah Wollaston said in the Commons debate: "It is no use having an embarrassed teacher who blushes when talking about sex and sexual violence. Often, the best educators are peer educators, particularly those who have been victims and are prepared to talk about the impact that has had on their lives."

How to be assertive

Aged 12-13, girls ought to have at least a few hours of tuition on how to be assertive when faced with difficult situations, such as street harassment. I do not mean to suggest the onus should be on girls to be able to defend themselves by means of a witty retort or a sharp kick in the knackers – although both of these methods have served me well on the long walk to womanhood. The goal should of course be to make sexual pestering and all forms of abuse unacceptable to both genders, but until such a utopia dawns, it makes sense to teach girls practical strategies, such as naming the behaviour (e.g. "That's very insulting", "You're invading my space") and removing yourself from the situation as quickly as possible. It might sound like simple and obvious stuff, but a surprising amount of adults, never mind young people, don't have the confidence to use this kind of language, or simply don't know what to do in a threatening situation.

Recognising sexual issues

Boys and girls in the 11-16 age group need at least a few hours of each school year devoted to relationship education, with single sex classes for certain topics where appropriate. The current PSHE syllabus needs to be expanded to include such things as the portrayal of women in the media, pornography, "sexting" and issues of personal respect and consent. Boys must be taught that "no" always means no, and outside agencies could be brought in to offer workshops in self-esteem for young people. Girls identified as being particularly vulnerable to abuse

or grooming – for example, those with behavioural or learning difficulties, and looked-after children, should be given individual support as a matter of course. Both sexes should be taught to recognise emotional abuse and controlling behaviour.

The importance of education

Some would argue that the proper place for sex and relationship education is within the family, rather than taking up valuable space on an already crowded curriculum, but many parents are simply unable to provide this. Lots of children grow up witnessing domestic violence or are victims of abuse themselves, and so have little idea what a healthy relationship even looks like. Financial education has been made statutory in schools, and yet there is resistance from the Government to legislate for proper relationship education. What does this say? That being able to handle your money with care is more important than being able to handle other people with care? That cash is king, men finish second, and women a distant third? I would suggest that teaching girls and boys how to relate well to one another and how to form respectful relationships might bring them far more happiness throughout their lives than any amount of A* grades ever could.

© The Independent, 4 March 2013
www.independent.co.uk

BOYS AND GIRLS IN THE 11 TO 16 AGE GROUP NEED AT LEAST A FEW HOURS OF EACH SCHOOL YEAR DEVOTED TO RELATIONSHIP EDUCATION WITH SINGLE SEX CLASSES FOR CERTAIN TOPICS WHERE APPROPRIATE

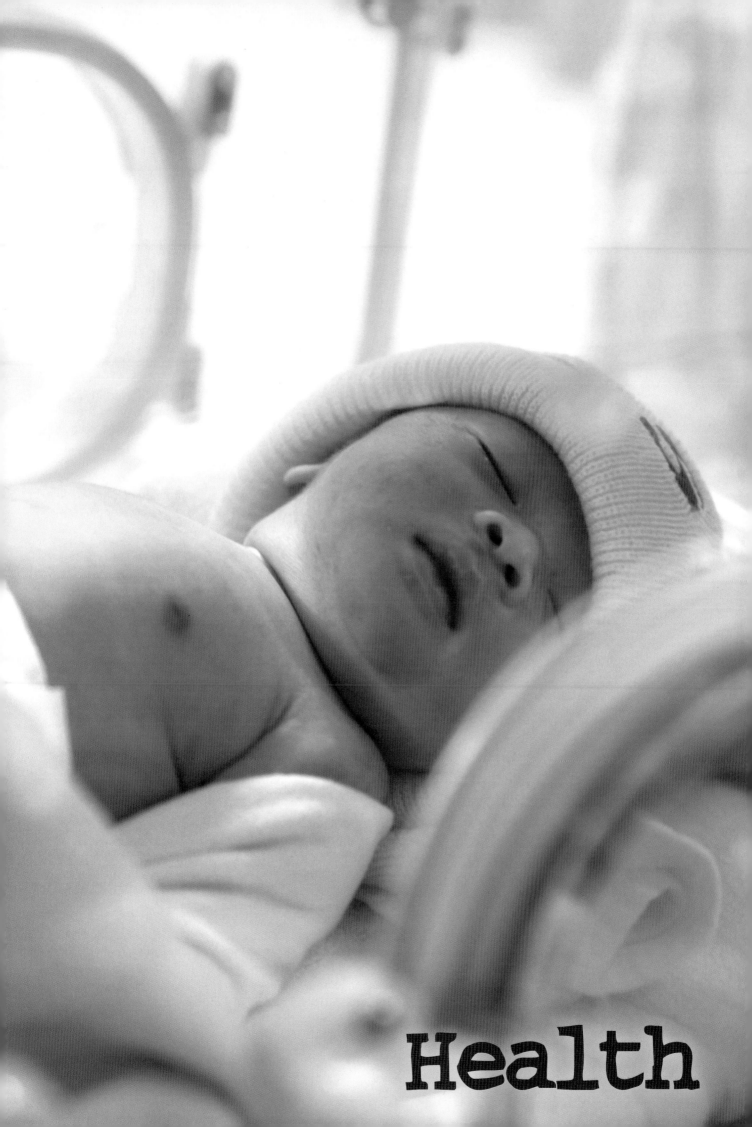

Health

I'VE SEEN THE AGONY OF ANOREXIA

Image courtesy of Vickie Townsend

BY JEMIMA LEWIS

SOME ISSUES:

Who do you think was responsible for taking care of Laura Willmott once she was over 18 years of age?

Should there be circumstances under which an adult is put into the care of another?

How would you have tried to help Laura?

See also:
Complete Issues
Body image and Eating disorders and Fact File 2014 for statistics about eating disorders

The newspaper pictures of Laura Willmott, who died aged 18 after starving herself down to five stone, show an exceptionally pretty young girl. Pretty and thin. Thin and pretty. Pretty, in part, because she was so thin.

One photograph shows her posing in what appears to be a strapless gold prom dress. Her hair is swept into a sophisticated up-do, her make-up is immaculate and, although her smile looks tired, her neat, heart-shaped face is beautiful. Her shoulders are shapely; her clavicles elegantly prominent. She looks Hollywood starlet-sized: enviably slender, not scarily so.

All of which just goes to show how warped is the lens of popular culture through which we view the female form. I don't know exactly when this photograph was taken, but Willmott – who battled against anorexia for five years before it killed her – was already very sick.

At Avon coroners' court this week, the awful narrative of her death was heard. As soon as she turned 18, Willmott discharged herself from the Child Mental Health Unit that had been treating her. Nine months later she could barely walk and was losing her hair.

"She became frailer and frailer," her mother told the court. "To get around the house at all she had to crawl."

Every time her parents took her to hospital, she discharged herself and, because she was officially an adult, the doctors allowed it. Even when she was in hospital, she lied to everyone, using tissues to soak up her nutrition drinks. Eventually, her body gave up: she had a cardiac arrest, which led to brain damage and then death.

Her parents say she was "doomed" from the moment doctors decided to treat her as an adult, cutting them out of decisions about her treatment. Perhaps they are right: NHS provision for mentally ill adults is often woeful, and anorexics of all ages are not noted for making sensible decisions about their own health.

AND WHO ELSE IS THERE TO BLAME, IF YOUR BELOVED, CLEVER, AFFECTIONATE CHILD TAKES IT INTO HER HEAD TO KILL HERSELF BY SLOW DEGREES?

And who else is there to blame, if your beloved, clever, affectionate child takes it into her head to kill herself by slow degrees? One of the cruelest aspects of anorexia is that the causes are still so little understood, leaving the parents – as is their natural reflex – to pick up the guilt.

The received wisdom is that it isn't really about food, but about a deeper unhappiness – probably, since its victims are so often young, rooted in childhood. Thus, the finger of blame swivels back to the parents. It is curious, though, that this particular expression of adolescent unhappiness only arises in cultures that worship thin women. Afro-Caribbean girls, though they doubtless have anxieties aplenty, have much lower rates of anorexia than white girls.

The desire to conform to an ideal of beauty can be dangerously strong: enough on its own, perhaps, to derail a young mind. I once had a friend whose younger sister suddenly – overnight, it seemed – stopped eating. Jessica was, until the anorexia set in, a gorgeous girl: 16, golden-skinned, with wild blonde curls and a spatter of freckles across her nose. She was never fat, not even in a puppyish way, but she wanted to be fashionably spindly. And once she began losing weight, it was too thrilling to stop.

Within six months, Jessica had reduced herself to a living cadaver. Her yellow skin seemed ready to peel away from her skull. The hair on her head was falling out, while a thick down had sprung up on her fragile limbs, like the simian fluff on a newborn baby. Too weak to walk, she spent her days stretched out on the playroom sofa, eyes closed and hands clasped, like the effigy of a medieval saint, ostentatiously fading away.

Normal family life becomes impossible when there's a suicidal liar in the house. I remember a particularly gruelling supper with Jessica's family. She was propped in a chair full of cushions to save her bones hurting, staring implacably at her plate while the rest of us tried to make polite conversation. Her mother kept begging her to eat,

waving dainty forkfuls under her nose as if she were a stubborn toddler. Her father – a gentle, dignified man in a cravat – sat at the end of the table with tears dripping off the end of his nose.

Anorexia is a solitary illness that nevertheless imposes itself violently on everyone close to the sufferer. It turns siblings into strangers, loving children into combatants, outgoing friends into miserable hermits.

The only thing worse than suffering from it yourself must be to see your child stolen away by it. Laura Willmott's parents have grief enough to bear. I hope they can resist the siren call of guilt.

A statement made by Vickie Townsend, the mother of Laura Wilmott, at the inquest into Laura's death

"I want to make it absolutely clear that I am not levelling blame at anyone. What I was terribly concerned about then and what I am equally concerned about now is the fact that it seemed to have been assumed that as Laura approached her 18th birthday that a) it was no longer appropriate for me to be copied into reports of her treatment and to be notified of missed appointments, ie evidence of her disengagement, and b) she was in a fit mental state then and immediately after she reached 18 to make decisions to whether she should engage with treatment at all.

"I strongly believe there is a gap in the provision of proper treatment here. It was obvious from Laura's history and her therapy, that although she'd made considerable progress in tackling her anorexia … she was by no means free of the condition. It was also obvious from her own acknowledgements and her refusal to be open-handed about measuring her progress that Laura was being deceitful to the professionals as well as to us. I struggled to see how Laura was any different at 17 years and 364 days than at 18 years and one day."

The Daily Telegraph, 23 February 2013
© Telegraph Media Group Limited 2013

Virginia Ironside's Dilemmas:

I need my mother by my side, how can I stand by and watch her die?

**My mum's refused another round of chemo,
even though it could give her another six months of life.
I feel so betrayed...**

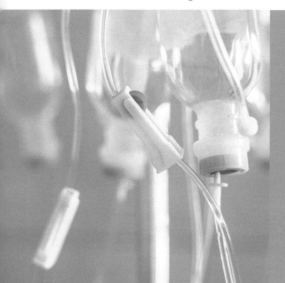

Dear Virginia,

My mum's had cancer for a few years, and chemotherapy, and now she's got secondaries and the doctors say if she has more chemo she might have another six months. But Mum's refused. She says she can't bear it and is happy to die. I'm at university, and just can't understand it. I feel so betrayed by her, and feel she should do anything to be with us a bit longer. My brother, who lives at home, says he understands, but my dad is in pieces. Is there any way we could persuade her? By the time six months is up they might have found a cure.

Yours sincerely, Rebecca

Virginia says ...

I'm afraid you have to face up to the sad truth, Rebecca. I can tell you categorically that there isn't going to be a cure found in six months. Your mother is going to die. Every person facing bereavement imagines there'll be a miracle cure and every one of them is disappointed. What you're trying to do is to put off the evil day when you lose your mother – and you're prepared to ask her to go through the most horrible effects of chemotherapy just to make things easier on yourself.

Your mother's already had chemotherapy. She knows what to expect. Your brother has probably witnessed her agonies and has understood that she can't bear to go through the pain, indignity and misery of this poisonous treatment with no chance of having anything more than a few more months. And what kind of months would they be anyway? Have you thought of that? She'd feel, probably, wretched and weak. Instead, she's taken the decision to live her short life to the full rather than stretching it out like some agonised piece of chewing gum. It's quality of time left she wants, not quantity.

SOME ISSUES:

Can you sympathise with the way this daughter feels?

What would you do if this were your mother?

Do you think Virginia Ironside's advice is correct or is she too harsh?

I've had lots of answers to this problem. Some readers suggest you take a sabbatical from university so you can spend this time with your mum. Many recommended Macmillan nurses. And one reader, wisely, recommended that you get your mother to make a living will or Advanced Directive, to be sure that when she gets nearer to dying, she can die peacefully and won't be given any painful resuscitation.

But the real problem with all this is timing. You haven't reconciled yourself to the fact that your mother's time has come. She, on the other hand, has come to terms with it. It's often difficult for people to understand that when it's time for them to go, the terminally ill often feel far calmer and more accepting of death than those around them. Trying to nag her into having more treatment will make your mother feel worse during her last months. Don't go on about it. You'll only feel dreadfully guilty later.

Pour out your feelings, instead, to a bereavement counsellor now, and try to make these last months of your mother's life the happiest they can be for her, so that this can be a time you to look back on with sadness, but also with reassurance that you put her feelings first and did your best for her in her last days.

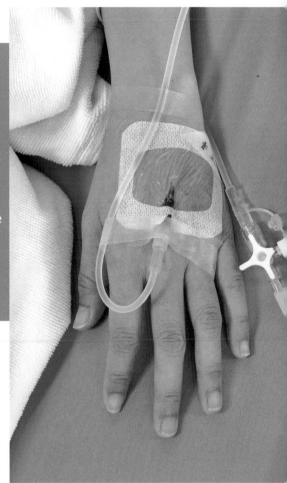

Readers say ...

Show her your love

I have been volunteering at a hospice for more than two years and I have seen so many times patients for whom the real battle is not facing death but having to deal with all the needs and baggage of those around them.

The most important gift that we can give to each other is freedom. And this is the ultimate freedom that your mother wishes to exercise now. Please don't try to deprive her of it. Enjoy those most precious of days left and use the opportunity to say and do all the things you've wanted to do together. You have a great chance to show her how much you love her.

Charlie, by email

Let her go

When my mother was diagnosed with cancer she refused the offer of an operation. She couldn't face it and was ready to die. It was so upsetting and we tried and tried to get her to change her mind. I remember saying to her that I wished I was 10 years old so she'd have to have the operation. After a time we realised we had to accept that it was her decision and move on to supporting and caring for her and you will, too. It is a terrible situation and I feel for you.

Jean, by email

'No! I Don't need Reading Glasses!'
by Virginia Ironside (Quercus £14.99)

© The Independent, 11 March 2013
www.independent.co.uk

You haven't reconciled yourself to the fact that your mother's time has come.

The NHS prioritising those with a 'healthy lifestyle'? I think there's enough stereotyping already

Bit tubby?
Back of the queue.

Smoker?
Back of the queue.

Drinker?
Back of the queue.

NATASHA DEVON

SOME ISSUES:

Do you think prioritising people with a 'healthy lifestyle' is fair?

What do you think counts as a healthy lifestyle?

Who has the right to say who should get treated first?

What would you do if you were in charge of the NHS?

Selected from Complete Issues:
How will we treat the wilfully ill?
*Essential Articles 15 p113
(see also Fact File 2014 for statistics on quality of care)*

Yesterday it was announced that a 'think-tank' has recommended that patients who have a 'healthy lifestyle' are prioritised for NHS care.

Here's why they're wrong:

Anyone who has had the misfortune to visit an A&E department recently will know that they aren't just stretched to capacity, they are stretched far beyond it. Medical professionals simply do not have time to conduct an in-depth health assessment of every patient who enters the building. Which inevitably means they'll have to rely on stereotyping, assumption and, ultimately, misdiagnosis.

And there's far too much of that going on already, as I recently discovered.

Last month my spleen ruptured for, as far as the doctors could make out, absolutely no reason whatsoever. This is, admittedly, an extremely unusual medical occurrence. However, I was shocked at the extent to which, during my week in a London hospital, assumptions about my health and lifestyle were made on a perfunctory, inaccurate and often purely visual basis and the words which actually came out of my mouth were completely disregarded.

I am almost six foot tall and a size 16. Whilst I'm not drastically overweight, the antiquated BMI chart tells a different story – I do have an absolutely almighty and disproportionate bosom. I have an active lifestyle (not rock climbing, marathon running type active, but I'm always dashing about at high speeds and rarely sit still), I eat a very healthy and balanced diet and I do not smoke. My vice-of-choice is that I'm partial to a tipple and, prior to my hospital visit, I drank about two large glasses of wine on an average night. The latter is a fact I was foolish enough to share, in a moment of ill-advised candour, with my A&E Doctor.

When I was admitted to hospital with extremely severe abdominal and shoulder pain, difficulty breathing and a visibly bloated stomach, the aforementioned doctor was quick to inform me that I had 'indigestion' because I 'drank too much' and gave me a little tiny pot of anti-burp medicine. When this, unsurprisingly, proved to be an inadequate remedy for my symptoms and scans revealed I did not have gall stones (from 'drinking too much') or appendicitis, I was placed 'under observation'.

Another doctor in the ward helpfully informed me that my stomach was not, in fact, as I had been insisting, bloated. Apparently she knew my body far better than I did. 'Just… you know', she said. (She followed this vague statement with a hand gesture I took to mean 'you're a little bit fat'). She recommended I

I drank about two large glasses of wine on an average night, a fact I was foolish enough to share, in a moment of ill-advised candour, with my A&E Doctor.

remained under observation. I insisted on having a diagnostic procedure. At no point during any of this was I considered to be 'urgent'.

I was put on a not-particularly-high-priority list. Two and a half days after being admitted to hospital I finally went in to have what I thought was a routine keyhole procedure to look inside my tummy with cameras.

Eight hours later I woke up. They'd found a litre and a half of internal bleeding in my abdomen (that'll explain the bloating, then) and had to perform an emergency laparotomy (where they slice you down the middle like a pirate would) to determine the source of the bleeding and eventually fix my broken spleen.

After my operation, I was told it would take me 'longer than most' to begin walking again because I'm a 'big girl'. I defied that broken logic and astounded my doctors and nurses by walking, lifting stuff and leaving the ward in record

time. A month later I am back to work, dashing about endlessly once more.

Despite the lazy stereotyping I was subjected to, my recovery proved that I am strong in both mind and body. Endless blood tests revealed me also to be in tip-top health.

Quite simply, if this proposed regulation is put into place then I and millions of others like me will be wrongly disadvantaged. Bit tubby? Back of the queue. Smoker? Back of the queue. Drinker? Back of the queue. Anyone who isn't a lean, glowing, gym-frequenting whippet who eschews anything known to reduce life-expectancy (including, presumably, stress), BACK OF THE QUEUE, because your ill health is clearly your own fault.

It's difficult enough trying to conquer the judgements already made about your lifestyle in medical circles, without it being enforced by official guidelines.

Two things stuck with me after my health-scare. The first is that had I listened to the initial advice I was given, or not been fortunate enough to be able to passionately stand up for myself and demand further investigation, I would now be dead.

The second is a comment by a family friend after the event, who said "do you think perhaps the doctors didn't take you seriously because you have pink hair?".

© *The Independent, 14 March 2013*
www.indpendent.co.uk

Despite the lazy stereotyping I was subjected to, my recovery proved that I am strong in both mind and body.

International Day of Happiness: Ways to turn that frown upside-down

By James Silcocks

Well everybody, today's the day. Finally, we have been provided with a one-off chance to put our miseries and anxieties to one side and embrace the spirit of cheerfulness, kindness and joy. Don't you feel happier already?

Well you should because today is the first 'International Day of Happiness', an event organised by the United Nations last summer to highlight the importance of wellbeing in a world that is otherwise dominated by financial woes, relentless self-interest and laborious daily routines.

Sounds great, right? Although a dedicated "day of happiness" may

others – and make both them and ourselves happy in the process.

I tend to find myself momentarily happier when somebody performs an act of kindness to help those around them. It helps to restore my otherwise ever-decreasing faith in humanity. Likewise, it cheers me up if I've done something which I know will make someone else happy. That's not to say that our kindness is motivated by self-interest; it's just a nice by-product of our actions.

Dr Mark Williamson, the Director of 'Action for Happiness' which is one of the

What can I do to celebrate the occasion and make the world around me a happier place?

SOME ISSUES:

Do you think International Happiness Day is a good idea?

What do you think can improve happiness?

How can people make themselves and others happier?

Why is this important?

Selected from Complete Issues:
Happy workers?
Fact File 2013 p186
(see also Fact File 2014 for more statistics on happy workers)

sound like a lovely idea in theory, you may find yourself wondering: what can I do to celebrate the occasion and make the world around me a happier place?

Our own sources of happiness can vary; you may be tempted to go out for a delicious meal, embark on a shopping spree, or even just laze around all day and relax. But the main focus of the International Day of Happiness is to direct our kindness towards

main organisations behind the International Day of Happiness, agrees. He suggests that even the smallest of positive actions can have a major impact on yourself and those around you.

"Extensive research shows that making other people happy activates the same reward sensors in your brain, so it's a win-win situation," Dr Williamson explains.

Even if you just hold a door open for someone, spare some change or simply smile at someone in the street, it can really make a difference.

"Even if you just hold a door open for someone, spare some change or simply smile at someone in the street, it can really make a difference. These ideas may seem trivial but they can transform our psychological health."

"Businesses should do more to prioritise the happiness of their workers too. It's been proven that the happier an employee is, the more likely they are to be motivated, productive, and form good working relationships," suggests Dr Williamson.

There we have it. We can make ourselves happier by making other people happier. If ever one needed additional reasons to be nice to others – besides the fact that it's simply the right thing to do – then that surely fits the bill.

So remember: hold doors open, offer your bus seats to the elderly, and put your spare change into charity boxes. And, to end on the cheesiest of lines, remember that if all else fails – a smile costs nothing.

Have a happy happiness day!

There we have it. We can make ourselves happier by making other people happier

Here are three suggestions for a happier life:

A – AFFIRM THE PLEDGE.
A simple act of adding your name to the thousands of others who have declared that they will "try to create more happiness in the world" around them.

C – CHEER 'HAPPY HEROES'.
Spreading the word on social network sites and paying tribute to those who go out of their way to make other people happy. Twitter users are encouraged to use the hashtag #HappyHeroes in their tweets.

T – TAKE PART ON THE DAY.
In addition to making others happy, there are numerous events going on around the world to celebrate the day, including a 'positive messages' flash mob at Liverpool Street Station.

For more information visit www.dayofhappiness.net

© The Independent, 20 March 2013
www.independent.co.uk

It's time to think big to tackle obesity crisis

Deanna Delamotta

SOME ISSUES:

Why do you think obesity is such a problem?

What causes obesity?

What can be done to help people who are obese?

Who should be responsible for dealing with obesity?

See also:
Complete Issues
Obesity

You can't pick up a newspaper without seeing Patsy Kensit, contorted at an odd angle extolling the virtues of WeightWatchers' New Approach – whatever that is. Does it involve eating less and exercising more by any chance?

A Slimming World leaflet plopped on my doormat yesterday just as I was about to reach for my son's selection box.

I took umbrage and chucked it into the overflowing recycling bin. How dare Janet from Slimming World assume I might be carrying around some surplus poundage. I don't know her but I dare say she won't be worried by my response as this is the busiest week of the year for slimming clubs, all vying to grab our flab and make it theirs.

You can't pick up a newspaper without seeing Patsy Kensit, contorted at an odd angle extolling the virtues of WeightWatchers' New Approach – whatever that is. Does it involve eating less and exercising more by any chance? And do we really need to pay over a fiver a week to discover this?

Slimming clubs are the traditional port of call for faint-hearted fat-fighters. You go along to a church hall or leisure centre and for the next six months you count calories or points and bore everyone rigid with how you are changing your eating habits for life not just post-Christmas – until you fall off the weight loss wagon into a bucket of chicken, fried in saturated fat.

But for the chronically obese, of whom there are an alarming number in this country – we're in the global silver medal position for fat – more drastic action is called for. Pam Pellegrinotti reckons Slimming World or WeightWatchers would have been too little too late for her when she tipped the scales at over 26st – massively obese for her 5ft 5in stature.

How dare Janet from Slimming World assume I might be carrying around some surplus poundage

The office manager from Crumpsall believed she wouldn't see her 40th birthday so spent £13,000 on a gastric bypass, reducing her tummy to the size of a boiled egg. She's now more than 14st lighter after funding her own weight loss odyssey – good for her – why should the NHS pick up the tab for a self-afflicted condition?

Look at Charlie Walduck, of Failsworth, who smashed the UK weight loss record, shedding over 30st in less

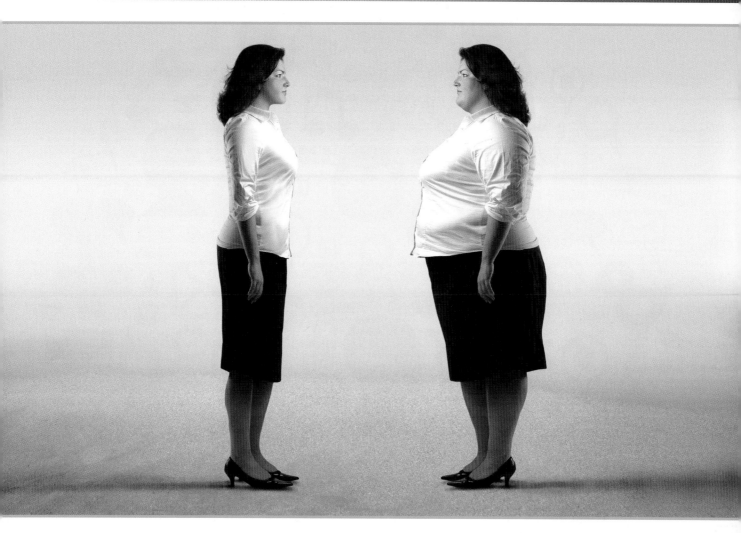

than two years without the aid of a gastric band, bypass or balloon. Sheer willpower won the day. But it's not as simple that. Charlie describes a constant battle

Obesity-related ailments are costing the NHS a massive £5bn a year

to keep his weight down, and to fight an underlying cause of his weight woes – depression.

Obesity-related ailments are costing the NHS a massive £5bn a year with

bariatric surgeons insisting it's more cost-effective to fund a one-off gastric bypass than years of health problems. And Pam's view that not enough is being done to help compulsive eaters is being echoed by health campaigners and Charlie who say GPs must help the obese rather than just telling them to cut down on fatty foods.

For an alarming number of us the margin between being an acceptable weight and obese is growing ever more slender. Tackling this epidemic requires political will although, as Charlie says: "It's not the government's fault people are overweight – it's people's fault". But like smokers and drinkers we can't just leave the obese

to eat themselves to death. Slimming clubs can't work in isolation from GPs and GPs need to see the big picture (excuse the pun) and start working collaboratively to help.

Because for every Charlie Walduck there are hundreds of 20, 30, 40 even 50st plussers stuck at home or in hospital with obesity-related ailments who are never going to find the will to diet. Paying for surgery to curb their cravings is a last resort after all other options have been exhausted as it may be the only way some overeaters are ever going to get a life – and stop costing us so dear.

Manchester Evening News,
3 January 2013

Internet and media

Hey advertisers, leave our defenceless kids alone

In-school marketing, promoting junk food online: how can we tolerate this corporate capture of young minds?

GEORGE MONBIOT

SOME ISSUES:

Do you think advertising companies should be able to advertise where they want to?

Why do you think advertising to pupils in schools might be a problem?

Is it fair to say if you do not like the advertising, just don't look? Or is advertising very hard to ignore in modern life?

Who should be responsible for where advertisements are allowed to appear?

How many people believe this makes the world a better place? A company called TenNine has hung hoardings in the corridors and common rooms of 750 British schools. Among its clients are Nike, Adidas, Orange, Tesco and Unilever. It boasts that its "high impact platform delivers right to the heart of the 11-18 year old market".

Other firms are closing in. Boomerang Media, which represents Sega, Atari, Virgin, Umbro and others, has persuaded schools to distribute Revlon perfume samples to their pupils. This campaign, it says, "was effectively linked into their PSHE and PE classes". PSHE means personal, social, health and economic education, or "learning to live life well". How the disbursement of perfume by teachers helps children to keep fit and live well is a mystery I will leave you to ponder.

Advertising in schools offers corporations a genuine captive market. Trade associations which defend the dark arts of persuasion argue that if you don't like advertisements, then you don't have to look at them. But in this case you do. While surveys suggest that roadside hoardings raise awareness of a company's products among 28% of the people who pass them, posters in schools, according to TenNine, reach over 80%.

Every year, advertisers press a little further into our lives, shrinking the uncontaminated space in which we may live. In ways of which we are often scarcely aware, they change our perceptions of the world, alter our values, infiltrate the language.

But at least adults have some defences. As the advertising executive Alex Bogusky points out, "children are not small grownups. Their brains are fundamentally different, the big difference being that right-hemisphere brain development doesn't really kick in until the age of 12. This is important because without the right hemisphere involved, all decisions and concepts are very black and white. If you sit with a child and watch TV commercials, you will notice how vigorously effective the messages are. 'I want that.' 'Can I have that?' 'I need that.' These words come out of their

mouths with seemingly every message, and they mean it and they believe it and they are defenceless against it."

These defenceless people are being pursued with precision and ruthlessness, and governments fail to protect them. In the United Kingdom advertisements for food high in fat, sugar or salt cannot be broadcast during children's television programmes. But they can be fired at children from UK websites. Nestlé, for example, has a "family" site in which children can "explore the fun" with Quicky the Nesquik bunny. There are prizes to win, jokes to share, games to play and TV adverts to watch. Cheestrings, making no pretence of reaching anyone other than young children, has a UK site called "101 fun things to do before you are 11½". Among them is "get fit fast", illustrated with the fatty, salty Cheestrings mascot.

The Sugar Puffs site, plainly targeted at children, invites them to "join in the fun", with jokes, computer games, electronic postcards to send to their friends and television ads promoting the junk the company sells. Disgracefully for the Variety Club charity, there's a cross-promotional page which uses the charity to push the Sugar Puffs brand. Surely the Variety Club is supposed to help sick children.

In his book Childhood Under Siege, Joel Bakan shows how computer games and social networking are being merged to create new advertising platforms. The aim, according to an executive he quotes, is to "get users in the door to play for free and then monetise the hell out of them once they're hooked". One way is to issue points or virtual coinage to kids who click on advertisements.

All this is promoted as fun and freedom. Parents who try to restrict children's access look like prudes and killjoys. "As our kids become immersed," Bakan notes, "in a [corporate] culture that works to pry them loose from us, we become less able to find the connection, respect, authority and credibility we need to keep them safe, healthy and in the long term happy."

In its coalition agreement, the government promised to "crack down on irresponsible advertising and marketing, especially to children". It commissioned a review that concluded that if advertisers failed to regulate themselves, the government should take action. The government says it agrees with "the thrust of all [the] recommendations".

> ...it's a marvel that we have for so long tolerated this capture of children's minds by companies exploiting their innocence and wonder

So where's the action? There's a website making it easier for parents to complain, and a promise by advertisers, already broken, not to use children as brand ambassadors or for peer-to-peer marketing. But on issues such as advertising in schools and the online promotion of junk food, not a word.

So it didn't take me long to decide to sign the open letter by a new campaign called Leave Our Kids Alone, asking for a ban on all advertising aimed at children under 11. It is long overdue: it's a marvel that we have for so long tolerated this capture of children's minds by companies exploiting their innocence and wonder. This is a campaign about more than advertising. It's about who we are: free-thinking citizens, raised on the best information and judgment that parents and teachers can provide; or captive consumers, suckled at home and at school on subtle corporate lies. I urge you to join it.

The Guardian, 15 April 2013
© Guardian News and Media Ltd 2013

The campaign Leave Our Kids Alone, asks for a ban on all advertising aimed at children under 11

www.leaveourkidsalone.org

Toddlers becoming so addicted to iPads they require therapy

Children as young as four are becoming so addicted to smartphones and iPads that they require psychological treatment.

Victoria Ward

Experts have warned that parents who allow babies and toddlers to access tablet computers for several hours a day are in danger of causing "dangerous" long term effects.

The youngest known patient being treated in the UK is a four-year-old girl from the South East.

Her parents enrolled her for compulsive behaviour therapy after she became increasingly "distressed and inconsolable" when the iPad was taken away from her.

Her use of the device had escalated over the course of a year and she had become addicted to using it up for to four hours a day.

Dr Richard Graham, who launched the UK's first technology addiction programme three years ago, said he believed there were many more addicts of her age.

"The child's mother called me and described her symptoms," he said.

"She told me she had developed an obsession with the device and would ask for it constantly. She was using it three to four hours every day and showed increased agitation if it was removed."

Dr Graham said that young technology addicts experienced the same withdrawal symptoms as alcoholics or heroin addicts,

SOME ISSUES:

Do you think there should be an age restriction on the use of iPads, phones and other gadgets?

Do you think iPads, phones and other gadgets can be addictive?

How much time do you think is 'healthy' to spend on such gadgets?

Selected from Complete Issues:
Great outdoors?
Fact File 2013 p28

One in seven parents admitted that they let children use the gadgets for four or more hours a day

when the devices were taken away.

He warned that the condition prevented young people from forming normal social relationships, leaving them drained by the constant interaction.

"Children have access to the internet almost from birth now," he told the Sunday Mirror.

"They see their parents playing on their mobile devices and they want to play too. It's difficult, because having a device can also be very useful in terms of having a reward, having a pacifier. But if you don't get the balance right it can be very dangerous.

"They can't cope and become addicted, reacting with tantrums and uncontrollable behaviour when they are taken away. Then as they grow older, the problem only gets worse. Even the most shy kids, when they hit their teens, suddenly want to become sociable and popular."

It is feared that products such as baby-proof iPad covers and iPotties, which

She became increasingly "distressed and inconsolable" when the iPad was taken away from her

feature built-in iPad stands, only fuel the problem.

Parents who have found themselves unable to wean their children off computer games and mobile phones are paying up to £16,000 for a 28-day "digital detox" programme designed by Dr Graham at the Capio Nightingale clinic in London.

Psychiatrists estimate that the number of people who have become digitally dependent has risen by 30 per cent over the past three years.

A survey last week revealed that more than half of parents allowed their babies to play with their phone or tablet device.

One in seven of more than 1,000 parents questioned by babies.co.uk website admitted that they let them use the gadgets for four or more hours a day.

James Macfarlane, managing director of the website, said: "Given that babies between 3-12 months are awake for only around 10 hours per day this is a huge proportion of their waking day.

"Although 81 per cent of our users felt that children today spend too much time on smart devices, it hasn't put most of them off using them to entertain their baby."

The Daily Telegraph, 21 April 2013
© Telegraph Media Group Limited 2013

It is feared that products such as baby-proof iPad covers and iPotties, which feature built-in iPad stands, only fuel the problem.

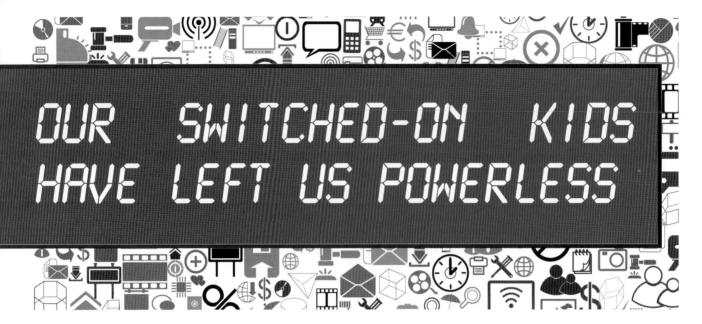

OUR SWITCHED-ON KIDS HAVE LEFT US POWERLESS

HOW ARE GROWN-UPS SUPPOSED TO COMPETE WITH THE LIKES OF NICK D'ALOISIO, THE 17-YEAR-OLD WIMBLEDON SCHOOLBOY WHO HAS JUST SOLD SUMMLY, HIS IPHONE APP, FOR £20 MILLION?

ALLISON PEARSON

SOME ISSUES:

Do you think children know more about technology than their parents?

Do you know more about it than the people you live with?

Is this a problem?

Are the older generation missing out?

Who should be responsible for a child's internet usage?

Selected from Complete Issues:
What good is information if our children can't understand it?
Essential Articles 13 p128

We have reached a point in human evolution where the main reason to reproduce is to make sure you have someone in the house who knows how to work the telly. At six minutes to 10, in living rooms up and down the land, a parent thinks they would like to see the news and points Remote Number 1 at an indifferent screen. At four minutes to 10, the same softly cursing parent scrabbles down the back of the sofa and triumphantly retrieves Remote Number 2.

They wiggle this second magic wand at the TV which now bears the hostile announcement: "No video signal." At one minute to 10, the hyperventilating parent has found a third remote under the cat, which they wave wildly (the remote, not the cat) while shouting like a coxswain in a Force 10: "Jack/Emily/Milly/Matthew, get in here NOW! I need to see the news. For God's sake, how hard can it be to put the TV on?"

Very hard. Practically impossible since the new sort came in. With its impenetrable HDM1, 2, 3 and 4 and the little AV thingy, which you have to press to get to the other thingies, technology is now so baffling that it is clear the elderly and middle-aged are being targeted in a sinister plot by the younger generation. How

else to account for the fact that locating Huw Edwards is well nigh impossible without a savvy 12-year-old on hand to roll his eyes in weary condescension, take the remote from you, turn it the right way up and press the correct button?

The little blighters are taking over a world in which you need at least two devices to operate a piece of equipment that used to turn on with a single switch, like a kettle. How are grown-ups supposed to compete with the likes of Nick D'Aloisio? The 17-year-old Wimbledon schoolboy has just sold Summly, his iPhone app, for a reported £20 million. Summly takes the journalism people like me work hard to research and write and crunches it down into 400 moronic characters. Sorry, accessible newsbites. I refuse to applaud this geek prodigy. Did the dinosaurs cheer the meteor that wiped them out?

Alas, there is no escape: Dinosaurs R Us. At a gathering of mums the other morning, one shamefaced woman admitted: "Sometimes, when I want to watch a film, I have to go and wake Alexander up and get him to do it for me." She was far from alone. Another mother confessed that her son had been banned from the Xbox after his accountant dad got a stonking bill for buying a virtual Wayne Rooney even more expensive than the real one.

The downside to Kid Who Knows How To Turn on Telly is that he or she can run rings round their parents. Just ask the poor Rowland-Frys. Eight-year-old Theo Rowland-Fry bought "virtual donuts" on his Simpsons iPad game. Whether you dunk a virtual donut, or eat them or blow them up, I have no idea, but with a few clicks

Mr Crossan blames Apple for duping his "sensible" son into buying games on his iPad, not realising he was clicking for extra "in-apps" (whatever they may be) which cost money. Apple has refused to cancel the horrendous charges, citing parental responsibility and pointing out that iPads "contain password locks to prevent accidental purchases".

Yeah, right. That'll stop Kid Who Can Read Passwords

Companies like Apple and other app-sellers are no better than honey-traps for unwary youngsters. If you are a parent reading this and thinking smugly, "That could never happen to us", I suggest you check your bank statements and Inbox. An email landed in mine this week congratulating me on paying to "rejoin Club Penguin". I have never, to my certain knowledge, joined a penguin club in the first place. Though I know someone who might have done.

"SOMETIMES, WHEN I WANT TO WATCH A FILM, I HAVE TO GO AND WAKE ALEXANDER UP AND GET HIM TO DO IT FOR ME." SHE WAS FAR FROM ALONE.

Theo racked up a bill of almost £1,000. Nick and Lisa Rowland-Fry only noticed when their bank account was empty.

This week, Doug Crossan, a policeman, revealed that he had reported his 13-year-old son Cameron for running up a £3,700 bill buying iPad games on his dad's credit card. Again, the parent didn't notice until he got a call saying he had a large outstanding debt. If a copper can't keep his child on the straight and narrow, what hope is there for the rest of us?

Upside-Down. We all dread our children going off the rails, but what if they're merrily racing along tracks we don't even understand? Has the generation gap ever been wider or more scary?

Or, as Summly would say: Techno Tots wipe out Dinosaur Mums.

The Daily Telegraph, 27 March 2013
© Telegraph Media Group Limited 2013

WHAT IF THEY'RE MERRILY RACING ALONG TRACKS WE DO NOT EVEN UNDERSTAND? HAS THE GENERATION GAP EVER BEEN WIDER OR MORE SCARY?

CAN COMPUTER GAMES SHARPEN YOUR MIND?

ANSWERING THE CALL OF DUTY MAY NOT BE EVERY STUDENT'S IDEA OF FUN, BUT YOU CAN PICK UP SOME VALUABLE SKILLS WHILE YOU CHILL OUT

JAMES PAVETT

SOME ISSUES:

Do you or your friends spend a lot of time playing video games?

Do you think video games are a distraction from studying?

Or can playing video games help you study better?

Are there any negative effects of playing video games?

Selected from Complete Issues:
The best solution to gaming addiction? Maturity and strategy
Essential Articles 15 p134

Finding a way to wind down in your spare time is crucial to getting through the stresses of university. Some students go for a walk, others like a drink. I like to take on wave after wave of murderous adversaries.

That's right, when I need to relax, I find solace in computer games. It might sound crazy, but I'm here to tell you that even that hour spent playing mini-golf online could be helping your studies in the long run.

A whopping eight out of 10 homes in the UK own a games console, and around 33.6 million people are gamers. I barely know anyone who doesn't own a games console or smartphone on which to play.

I admit that almost every moment I'm not studying, sleeping or eating I am engaging in some form of video game. But could this "wasted time" be helping me?

One study, completed in 2010, looked at the effect of playing different violent video

up these skills while plundering dungeons for loot!

I asked my fellow gamers whether they thought video games benefited them academically. The response was mixed, varying from: "I wish I'd never started

I ADMIT THAT ALMOST EVERY MOMENT I'M NOT STUDYING, SLEEPING OR EATING I AM ENGAGING IN SOME FORM OF VIDEO GAME.

games on young adults and argued that they "reduce depression and hostile feelings in players through mood management" and help them cope better with stress. The researchers acknowledged that this probably wouldn't come as a surprise to gamers. It doesn't.

As little as an hour of game play helps me go back to work with a newly focused and clutter-free brain, ready to tackle the mammoth task of essay writing.

Problem-solving games are particularly good. Playing a few levels of a simple puzzler allows me to take my mind off an essay question, meaning I can go back to it without stale ideas rattling around my head.

As for proofreading, this study from the University of Rochester in the US found that playing computer games for a few hours each day improves people's ability to recognise letters. This demonstrates how video games can help you focus on finer details. Like naughty little misplaced apostrophe's.

You don't have to fly solo. Playing with friends can increase the stress-relieving qualities, and make for a great social night in.

I regularly play with a small group of friends and our games of choice always involve a high level of teamwork and co-ordination. Indeed, playing with friends can help you develop a surprising number of those transferable skills beloved of CV-readers: co-operation, communication, money management, critical thinking, decision-making under pressure. And you're picking

playing" to "I'm on a game-programming course, it's kind of essential". But the general consensus could still be summed up in a single word – escapism. We all agreed that on that score, video games couldn't be beaten.

So if you're looking for a way to slip out of your busy schedule and refresh your mind, look no further than your Xbox. There's nothing like a killer zombie when it comes to putting things in perspective

The Guardian, 20 March 2013
© Guardian News and Media 2013

AS LITTLE AS AN HOUR OF GAME PLAY HELPS ME GO BACK TO WORK WITH A NEWLY FOCUSED AND CLUTTER-FREE BRAIN, READY TO TACKLE THE MAMMOTH TASK OF ESSAY WRITING.

The power of the drug cartels has forced Mexico's media into silence – so Blog del Narco's voice is more essential than ever

Why BLOG DEL NARCO

has become the MOST IMPORTANT WEBSITE in Mexico

In 2010, the birth year of the popular and controversial website Blog del Narco, Mexico's tumultuous drug war reached a turning point. Monterrey, an economic engine of the country and once famously known as the safest city in Latin America, was engulfed by narco blockades and gun battles. In the neighboring state of Tamaulipas, the leading gubernatorial candidate was assassinated, and the border cities of Camargo and Mier became ghost towns.

In the first two months of 2010, eight journalists were kidnapped in the border city of Reynosa. The offices of news organizations across northern Mexico were attacked with grenades and strafed with gunfire. Only two of the kidnapped reporters survived. When the reporters returned to their newsroom at El Milenio in Mexico City, their editor, Ciro Gomez Lleyva, wrote what was essentially the obituary for press freedom in his country. "In more and more regions of Mexico, it is impossible to do journalism. Journalism is dead in Reynosa, and I have nothing more to say."

As Mexico's media outlets stopped reporting on the cartels and the government remained silent, Blog del Narco, launched in March 2010, began to fill the void. The blog featured raw photos and videos of executions, and gun battles uploaded by anonymous contributors. Within months, Blog del Narco was one of the most visited websites in Mexico with 3m monthly visitors. The blog documented the drug war in all its horror: photos of decapitated heads, mutilated torsos and other stomach-jarring acts of violence committed by organized crime to induce terror among the population.

Frightened and curious Mexicans read Blog del Narco to understand what was happening to their country. "We were living in some kind of low-intensity war," said Guadalupe Correa-Cabrera, an associate professor at the University of Texas at Brownsville who studies organized crime in her native Mexico. "We had never seen houses burnt, people massacred like this before. It was deeply frightening."

Anonymity became the only safeguard for freedom of expression. Blog del Narco posted every grim corpse photo and every gory account of assassination without attribution. It was unclear whether the stories

SOME ISSUES:

How do you think the drug gangs have gained control in Mexico?

Why can't the law sort out the situation?

What does Blog Del Narco demonstrate about the power of the internet?

Why is it important for people to know what is really happening where they live?

See also:
Complete Issues
Drugs

The cartels tried to dispatch Blog del Narco much like they had Mexico's other media outlets.

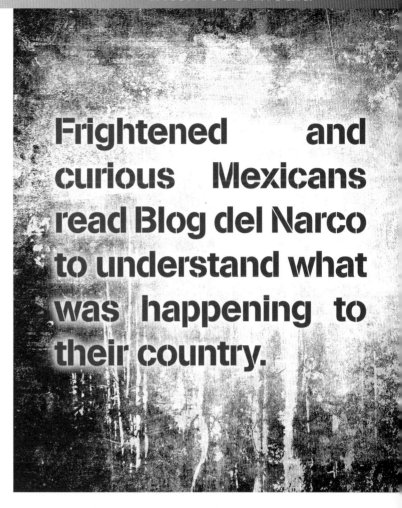

Frightened and curious Mexicans read Blog del Narco to understand what was happening to their country.

were ripped from other websites or were original reporting. And it seemed like no moderator existed. "The site was a mess," Correa-Cabrera said.

But everyone read it anyway. It was gruesome, but the violence needed to be documented, because it was happening. "If anything, Blog del Narco is an account of the facts. Proof that it happened. Because if we do not acknowledge what is happening in our country, then we can never change it," Correa-Cabrera said.

The cartels tried to dispatch Blog del Narco much like they had Mexico's other media outlets. The blog suffered hundreds of cyber-attacks. Anonymous and unsubstantiated rumors began to circulate that the site favored one cartel over another. In 2011, the website suffered a debilitating cyber-attack and was offline several days before it switched servers. Then a man and a woman were killed and hung from a bridge in the border city of Nuevo Laredo, with a sign warning that they had been killed for working on anonymous websites like Blog del Narco. "This is what will happen to all the internet snitches. Be warned: we are watching you. Sincerely Z [Los Zetas]."

Since the dark days of 2011 and the crippling cyber-attack, Blog del Narco has redoubled its efforts. The authors' first book, Dying for the Truth: Undercover Inside the Mexican Drug War, published by Feral House, is now on sale. In the book, written in Spanish and English, the anonymous authors of the blog document the dissolution of their country in 2010 by starting with an apology: "We are well educated and don't tend to curse, but we're going to say this because it's the way it is: our country is fucked. It has been for a long time."

The book is divided into short chapters that report month by month the bloody battle for territory by organized crime during 2010 and the first two months of 2011. The photos are as gruesome, and as graphic, as they are on the website. The text gives concise explanations of events, including transcriptions of narco messages left behind on the bodies.

Nothing in the book is attributed. Some of the chapters are remarkably detailed. In one chapter titled Gubernatorial Candidate is Murdered with His

Team Members, the authors explain how Rodolfo Torre Cantú, Tamaulipas's leading gubernatorial candidate for the Institutional Revolutionary Party, or PRI, was ambushed in June 2010 by Los Zetas cartel outside the state's capital. The chapter describes how the hitmen slept in a motel near the ambush site, and how the cartel's leader at the time, Heriberto Lazcano Lazcano, personally supervised the massacre of Torre and his campaign team. Three graphic photographs in the book document the massacre.

Three years later, the gubernatorial candidate's murder, like thousands of others in the past six years, has yet to be investigated by Mexican authorities. The country's new president Enrique Peña Nieto, anxious to suppress the growing conflict, is increasingly adopting a policy of silence. Gone are the press conferences touting the deployment of more troops or the capture of a drug kingpin that were common under the previous president, Felipe Calderón. Attacks against the press are once again on the rise, and recent gun battles raging across northern Mexico are scarcely reported by the media.

Someday, when the violence ends, historians won't have much information to help explain the bloodiest era in the country's history since the Mexican Revolution. What they will have is Blog del Narco.

• *Melissa del Bosque is a staff writer at the Texas Observer, specialising in immigration and border issues*

Texas Observer, 3 April 2013

WASSUP?

How we get shamazing new words

Despite the influence of dictionaries, outraged people who write to the papers and, yes, teachers, it's never simple to say what is right and what is wrong where language is concerned.

Language – particularly the English language – is not fixed. It is constantly changing in response to new inventions, changes in our lifestyle and manipulation by business and advertising (as in the Budweiser campaign that made 'Wassup' cool). And as the pace of our lifestyle increases, so too does the introduction of new words.

How new is new?

That word 'lifestyle' was first used 1939. It only came into more common use from 1991 – does that make it a new word or an old one? Very old words often change or expand their meaning. The word 'community', for example, has been used since the Middle Ages for a group of people living together but has more recently been extended to apply to people with a similar lifestyle (how did we ever manage without that word!) or mindset (first used 1909), as in 'the gay community' or 'the cycling community'.

Now, thanks to the internet, there is a 'community' of people who can live thousands of miles apart and have never actually met but feel like 'friends'. And it is the internet that is responsible for the invention and spread of a large number of new words.

Before 2001 we couldn't 'google' anything and it wasn't till 2004 that early adopters could 'facebook' their 'friends' (remember when you used to 'poke' people?). Those are both examples of something that happens naturally in language - a proper noun became a useful verb.

When Twitter arrived in 2006 it brought its own verb, to tweet, and introduced us to the hashtag. In that same year, the edition of Merriam-Webster's Collegiate® Dictionary included new words such as: ringtone, spyware, drama queen, unibrow, supersize and manga.

What now?

Perhaps inevitably once we had smartphones we needed the word 'dumbphone' for phones that just ... phone people. Like dumbphone, 'flexitarian' – a partial vegetarian, is being considered for entry into the dictionary. 'Omnishambles' was named the Word of the Year for 2012, it refers to a situation

SOME ISSUES:

Do you think making up words is good for the language or bad?

Is it important that a language keeps on changing?

Should a language represent the lives and culture of its people?

What words do you and your friends use that are made up?

See also:
Contrariwise p141

Selected from
Complete Issues:
For the latest way to say
'I love you' simply try 459
Essential Articles 12 p147

Before 2001 we couldn't 'google' anything and it wasn't till 2004 that early adopters could 'facebook' their 'friends'

that has been completely mismanaged. 'Frenemy' and 'amazeballs' also got the dictionary seal of approval

The 2012 Olympics established 'medalled' as a verb so that "She medalled in the last Olympics, will she medal in this one?" refers to someone's chances of winning rather than the prospect of them turning the games into an omnishambles by their interference.

This has now been joined by 'to podium'. But, given how well Britain's sportspeople did, it's hard to deny them an extra verb – even an ugly one. And it does save the commentators some time.

A word has to be useful for it to last. Presumably 'onesie' will only last as long as the fashion does while 'selfie' (a photo you take of yourself to put on a social network) could stick around. Some new words add extra meaning. 'Jel', especially in 'Well jel', expresses a softer sentiment than just jealousy – envy combined with admiration, perhaps.

New words can be quickly discredited if used by the 'wrong' people. X-factor judge Nicole Scherzinger coined 'shamazing;' to describe a

performance but its chances of being widely used were surely ruined when it was borrowed by the Prime Minister. In texting nothing predicts the death of a phrase more certainly than the moment the 'rents' start to understand and use it - so YOLO could be doomed.

So what's next?

According to the Future Laboratory some of the words we will need to describe tomorrow's lifestyles (there it is again!) will include 'Child Technology Officers' - tiny 'digital natives' (first use around 2001) who will know more than their parents about technology. They will grow into 'Screenagers' for whom virtual and actual life are the same. Probably these already exist, as do 'Sharents' who tweet and post every new detail and photograph of their darling child.

Over to you...

So how do you make new words? You can begin by shortening phrases to their letters - like laser and lol. You can make them by borrowing a noun and using it as a verb, as we do when we hoover. You can combine an accepted prefix with a new word - like microblogging. You can make a mash-up (2001-ish) like brunch or chillax.

Why not go ahead and make some of your own? Shakespeare is credited with creating 1,700 new words. Your word could become fashionable (Shakespeare), it could be majestic (Shakespeare) or zany (Shakespeare). Or it could be simply shamazing (Scherzinger)!

Source: Various

contrariwise

words that are their own opposites

As if the English language isn't difficult enough!

We have multiple ways of spelling the same sound. We have spellings that look the same but are pronounced differently. We have a vast vocabulary of words with similar meanings but slightly different nuances... **and we also have a whole host of words that can function as their own opposites.**

left Take that everyday word "left", for example. Depending on the rest of the sentence it can refer to someone who has gone or someone who has stayed behind. "When Ann left the room, only Thomas was left."

Fast can mean moving quickly or standing still: "He ran as fast as he could but still found himself stuck fast in the clinging mud." **fast**

bound Similarly I could be moving towards a destination "Bound for Liverpool" or unable to move "Totally bed-bound".

When you fix something you solve a problem yet when you are in a fix your problem remains. **fix**

bolt To bolt can mean to secure something or it can mean to escape "The horse has bolted" - a contrast illustrated in the old pun "He made a bolt for the door."

Even the simple preposition "with" can contradict itself: "I fought with him against the others, then I fought with him about my share" **with**

off And "off" can imply either not working or working: "I thought I had turned the alarm off but it still went off".

Something as simple as a hyphen can completely reverse the meaning. A footballer who resigns leaves his team while one who re-signs continues to play for it.

There are whole phrases whose meaning can be totally different. When I tell you "It's all downhill from here" I'm forecasting either a deteriorating situation or an easier ride. When I promise to "take care" of someone should they expect protection or defend themselves against my attempt on their life?

And, of course we take delight in making things their opposite. Want to say something is outstandingly good? You could always say it's sick or just bad.

Source: Various

SOME ISSUES:

Do you think the English language is confusing?

Should words that sound the same be spelt the same?

Do things like contradictory word meanings make the English language hard to understand?

See also:
Wassup? p139

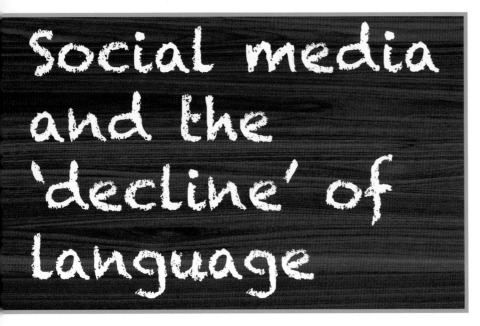

Social media and the 'decline' of language

"Most people who bother with the matter at all would admit that the English language is in a bad way". How often have you heard something similar – the opinion that texting, Twitter and Facebook are corrupting their (mainly) young users, leaving them barely able to construct a sentence and completely ignorant of the normal patterns of English spelling. If that is the case, the future for English looks grim.

But that opening quote is actually the first sentence of George Orwell's famous essay "Politics and the English Language", written in 1946, long before anyone could have imagined such a thing as a world wide web, when the term 'social media' would have been completely meaningless. The complaint was not new even in Orwell's time. You could go back to the ancient Greeks and find examples of people worrying about the language being corrupted – along with young people being lazy and disrespectful to their elders.

So is change a #badthing?

For some people new ways of writing, like 'lol' and 'l8r', are like graffiti on the walls of a cathedral – brutally defacing the beauty of the past. They despise the conversational, informal exchanges on Facebook. They argue that, since spelling and grammar can be disregarded in a tweet or a Facebook post, the same inaccuracy will seep into more formal writing. When young people see no reason to abide by the rules of language, chaos, or at least bad grammar, will reign.

The critics also have another, deeper point. In his novel, Nineteen Eighty-Four, Orwell invented a language called Newspeak. This was one of the tools of oppression – manipulating the way people thought by dumbing-down language and removing choices. An official of the dictatorship explains:

"Take "good", for instance. If you have a word like "good", what need is there for a word like "bad"? "Ungood" will do just as well – better, because it's an exact opposite, which the other is not. Or again, if you want a stronger version of "good", what sense is there in having a whole string of vague useless words like "excellent" and "splendid" and all the rest of them? "Plusgood" covers the meaning, or "doubleplusgood" if you want something stronger still."

For a dictatorship, limiting language makes alternative modes of thought impossible. Taking away options and choices in words removes the ability to range widely in your thoughts, to register and empathise with complex emotions or to be creatively different.

Critics of social media argue that people are voluntarily adopting this restricted mode of speech and thought: by using the shorthand of a hashtag or an emoticon we reduce and coarsen the expression itself, the reader's response and the thinking process. Surely only the broadest emotions can be expressed in a smiley, crying or winking face? And if we never articulate subtle shades of feeling, will there be a time when we lose the ability to feel them?

SOME ISSUES:

Do you think the use of the internet and emails have made you write more?

Do you write differently in emails and online than you do when writing essays?

Which style of writing best reflects how you like to speak?

What are the advantages to writing as if you were speaking?

What could be the disadvantages?

Selected from Complete Issues:
Mind your language
Essential Articles 12 p144

If you have something of value to say or a real insight to deliver, can you really do that in 140 characters on Twitter? Or is it only suited to giving an insight into what you had for dinner: 'Bangers and mash #nomnomnom' with an instagram of the meal. The expansion of trivial communication through social media will bring about the death of both language and thought.

But are they right? ☺

Are young people really reduced to being only semi-literate as a result of new means of communication? The skills used in texting: deducing from initial letters, understanding phonetic structures, use of context to decipher meaning, are the same as those used in conventional reading, writing and spelling. In actual fact, studies have found that in order to use an abbreviation like 'l8r' or 'hmwrk' youngsters need to be aware of the meaning and structure of the original word. This generation may be the most literate ever as they are continually engaging with the written word. They are constantly reading and writing, not 'War and Peace', admittedly, but blogs, tweets, posts and texts.

Not only that, but since so much of their writing is public, they will be very quickly corrected when a misspelling causes confusion or a badly chosen word causes offence. Since the responses are instant, writers have the chance to correct their work even after it is first 'published'. The written word, which was once a permanent record, is now changeable, fluid and more like a conversation than a lecture. For writers of blogs and of fiction, the chance to interact with their audience is an invaluable (and often painful) experience.

And far from encouraging triviality, the very shortness of tweets means they have to be concise, with no irrelevance, no rambling. The restriction forces you to think about what you really want to say and the most precise way to say it.

Not only are social media giving more opportunities for writing they are encouraging the development of different styles or voices. Just as you would speak differently in a variety of social situations, you write differently in the different media. For example, Facebook and LinkedIn are both used to connect with people but their tones are different. As a business network, LinkedIn requires full sentences, conventional language, a more formal, professional approach than Facebook's casual, chatty style. The same people use both media, but the audience, the intention and therefore the language they use will be different.

A unique feature of these media is the ability for large groups of people to collaborate instantaneously and spontaneously on projects. Wikipedia is the most famous example of this crowd-sourced knowledge. Another example is The Urban Dictionary, www.urbandictionary.com, which defines new words and phrases, often in a humorous (or crude) way. Describing itself as 'the dictionary you write' and inviting

you to 'Define your world', it has had a staggering 7 million entries since 1999. Amongst them is a concise example of the different content and styles of different media:

> **Facebook:** I like eating doughnuts.
>
> **Twitter:** I am eating #doughnuts.
>
> **Instagram:** Here is a Polaroid-esque photo of doughnuts.
>
> **YouTube:** Here I am eating doughnuts.
>
> **LinkedIn:** My skills include doughnut eating.
>
> **Pinterest:** Here is a recipe for doughnuts.

So are social media exchanges a threat or a development? We all know that change is inevitable, after all, we don't speak or write in the language of Shakespeare or Dickens or even Orwell. There is no previous example of language being shared, re-invented and adapted so quickly, by so many people. Changes now are not passed down by Orwell's Big Brother but rise up from the street – not a language dictatorship but a language democracy.

Sources: Various

PUNCTUATION FOR THE NATION: WHY WE NEED TO KEEP THE APOSTROPHE

The apostrophe exists to eliminate confusion, not to cause it. If we call something St Pauls Square, rather than St Paul's Square, will future generations assume there was more than one St Paul?

Paul Taylor

Photo: Bikeworldtravel Shutterstock.com

In the week we get a Budget, a Cypriot economic calamity and the inauguration of a new Pope, I thought I would focus on the really big news: a victory for the humble apostrophe.

The tiddler of the punctuation world was due to be purged from the street signs of Mid Devon by order of some local government suits who, frankly, should have better things to do.

These meddling bods feared that calling a road King's Drive or St George's Avenue was a recipe for "potential confusion", and so to spare apostrophobes from a concept they should really have learned about at primary school, the council proposed to ban all punctuation from road names.

Cue a mighty uprising of punctuation crusaders and even an editorial in the Times. Leader of Mid Devon council Peter Hare-Scott then overturned the batty idea, perhaps fearing that once they had purged the apostrophe, the punctuation police would come gunning for his hyphen.

The apostrophe exists to eliminate confusion, not to cause it. If we call something St Pauls Square, rather than St Paul's Square, will future generations assume there was more than one St Paul? Or that there was an individual called St Pauls? And if we remove one apostrophe to make life easier, doesn't it make it that bit more difficult to understand all the other punctuation in our everyday life?

Lynne Truss, author of Eats, Shoots and Leaves, showed what difference properly-placed punctuation makes to a

SOME ISSUES:

Do you think it is easy to understand what an apostrophe is for?

Do you think that road and shop signs should always use the apostrophe correctly?

Does it matter?

When might it cause confusion?

What other grammatical errors might affect understanding of shop and road signs?

"THE GIRLS LIKE SPAGHETTI" IS A SIMPLE STATEMENT ABOUT CERTAIN FEMALES' CULINARY PREFERENCES "THE GIRL'S LIKE SPAGHETTI" IS WHAT YOU SAY ABOUT A SUPERMODEL

I won't be joining the Apostrophe Protection Society any time soon; I do like to do my bit for the continued survival of the semicolon, however. Years ago, my wife did favour direct action, taking out a pen and correcting misuse of the apostrophe on the notice board at our sons' primary school (and bear in mind that that last apostrophe tells you in an instant that we have more than one son).

You really would expect a school to get these things right. But then you would expect the same of one of the nation's favourite book sellers. Yet Waterstone's became Waterstones 12 months ago – a concession to the world of URL addresses and email in which the apostrophe is as welcome as a wet dog at a wedding reception.

Apostrophiles may wish to bring some commercial pressure to bear by spending their money only in places which preserve this endangered species.

sentence. "The girls like spaghetti" is a simple statement about certain females' culinary preferences. "The girl's like spaghetti" is what you say about a supermodel.

But Mid Devon council was not the first, nor will it be the last, to consider the apostrophe as a bit of lexical scurf to be swept away for fear of making English look messy. For years, big corporations have been banning apostrophes just as energetically as greengrocers have been putting them where they don't belong.

Although we are now obliged to call it House of Fraser, there was a long period when the department store on Deansgate which used to be Kendal, Milne & Co was called an apostrophe-free Kendals. Come to think of it, the firm was purging punctuation even longer ago, witness the carving of the legend Kendal Milne & Co, minus comma, in marble above the store's main entrance.

And that's got me thinking about whether Deansgate ever had an apostrophe in the middle...

TAKING OUT A PEN AND CORRECTING MISUSE OF THE APOSTROPHE ON THE NOTICE BOARD AT OUR SONS' PRIMARY SCHOOL (AND BEAR IN MIND THAT THAT LAST APOSTROPHE TELLS YOU IN AN INSTANT THAT WE HAVE MORE THAN ONE SON).

In which case, you would need to give Selfridges, Currys, Harrods and Morrisons a wide berth, but would find this one of those rare instances when McDonald's is the ethical choice.

Manchester Evening News, 20 March 2013

Law & order

MRS JUSTICE THIRLWALL:

THE ONE WOMAN PHILPOTT COULDN'T DEFEAT

Thirlwall issued a judgement so razor-sharp that when I read the full transcript I felt like punching the air

GRACE DENT

Photo: Elizabeth Cook/PA Wire/Press Association Images

Mick Philpott was sentenced to life in prison for the manslaughter of six of his children in a house fire. His wife Mairead and friend Paul Mosley were both given a 17 year sentence. The couple started the fire at their Derby home in a failed plot to frame Lisa Willis, Mick Philpott's former girlfriend.

Some politicians said the case proved that living on benefits was a lifestyle choice.

SOME ISSUES:

Do you think the judge's background can affect a case?

Why do you think there are not more female judges in the UK?

Why are details raised by this judge essential to a criminal case?

See also:
Complete Issues
Law

It's rare that I feel spirited by news from the British court system, but this week, during the summing-up of the Philpott trial by Mrs Justice Thirlwall, a small gut-punch of hope startled me.

It was the day on which the nation – including George Osborne, various voiceboxes of the left and several radio phone-ins – were in furious debate over whether Mick Philpott's benefit handouts had led to the deaths of six children.

Would Mick Philpott have been a less bleak individual if someone from the Job Centre had appeared by his pillow each morning with a clipboard/truncheon and chivvied him off to

> BEFORE EXAMINING THE NIGHT IN QUESTION THIRLWALL SAID: "IT IS NECESSARY TO LOOK AT THE HISTORY OF YOUR RELATIONSHIP WITH WOMEN." I'VE RARELY HEARD A JUDGE SAY SUCH A THING

pick litter? Did benefits lead to him creating this "doomed brood"? Remember, having five or six kids if they're all dressed in Boden eating Jamie Oliver recipes from your outdoors kiln is a charming status symbol. If they're clad in cast-offs and eating out of the Whoops! section in Asda, they're "a feral brood" that must be stopped.

Still, we pondered, would Mick Philpott have been less likely to set fire to a house in a twisted attempt to frame his ex-girlfriend for arson if he'd had less money for groceries? This raised the question – although I was reluctant to add to the quacking – of how Fred West*, a successful builder, committed any acts of violence at all, what with the devil only making work for idle hands.

I mention West because the summing-up by Mrs Justice Thirlwall – whom you may have noticed to be a female judge – raised in my mind several stomach-churning similarities between the two cases. Thirlwall issued a judgement so razor-sharp that when I read the full transcript I felt like punching the air. Because while the nation bickered about Philpott's access to housing benefit, Thirlwall spelled out the true matter at hand about Philpott's systematic campaigns reaching back over 40 years of violence, mental abuse, manipulation and blackmail against vulnerable women. She spelled out why many men like Philpott – regardless of class – have multitudes of children. Thirlwall was determined there would be no neat summations of Philpott's unfortunate "mistake" in 2012, because this was a far longer, detailed story that needed telling.

Before examining the night in question – the petrol, the plot, the screaming 999

> IT'S TINY DETAILS LIKE THIS THAT ONLY JUDGES FROM DIVERSE BACKGROUNDS CAN PICK UP ON. WHEN MEN LIKE PHILPOTT WASH UP IN COURT I WISH THERE WERE MORE WOMEN LIKE THIRLWALL TO MEET HIM AND JAIL HIM FOR LIFE

Photo: Rui Vieira/PA Archive/Press Association Images

ONLY 15.5 PER CENT OF HIGH COURT JUDGES ARE WOMEN. THE ODDS WERE AGAINST PHILPOTT MEETING A FEMALE JUDGE THIS WEEK – ONE WOMAN HE HAD NO CHANCE OF CONTROLLING, STRIKING, OR IMPREGNATING – BUT I'M QUIETLY JOYOUS HE DID.

calls, the dead children – Thirlwall said: "It is necessary to look at the history of your relationship with women." I've rarely heard a judge say such a thing, although in the judicial system there aren't that many female judges, so there's more chance this take on events is overlooked. Across Europe, the average gender balance among judges is 52 per cent men and 48 per cent women. At 23 per cent, England and Wales is fourth from the bottom, followed only by Azerbaijan, Scotland and Armenia. The higher up the court system, the more male-dominated the bench becomes. Only 15.5 per cent of High Court judges are women. The odds were against Philpott meeting a female judge this week – one woman he had no chance of controlling, striking, or impregnating – but I'm quietly joyous he did.

Thirlwall recounted that Mick Philpott almost killed two women when he was a soldier in his twenties – employed, you might note, not remotely on benefits. Philpott was a violent and jealous boyfriend, at one point breaking his young girlfriend's arm, another time smashing her leg with a sledgehammer.

Eventually his jealousy led to him breaking into her house, stabbing her repeatedly in a ferocious attack and then turning the knife on her mother. "You have, I am rightly reminded, served your sentence for that, but it is clear from the evidence that I excluded from the trial that you have used that conviction as a means of controlling women, terrifying them in what you might do."

Thirlwall dissected the kingly rule that Philpott had over his first wife (unnamed), then Heather Kehoe, a 16-year-old he left this wife for when he was in his forties, then Mairead Philpott, then Lisa Willis. A crucial idea – seen commonly in abuse cases and until now rarely spoken of – is

Philpott's yearning to keep all of these women almost perpetually pregnant. Babies and more babies. Seventeen babies. Not bred to milk the benefits system. Bred so his girlfriends and wives cannot look or move elsewhere when they're rotund and vulnerable. Bred in tribute to his enormous prowess and machismo. Followed, time and again, by court cases at Philpott's behest to remove custody of babies from his ex-wives and girlfriends. Taking children from their mothers was Philpott's ultimate tool of power, after mental and physical cruelty. "Women were your chattels," said Justice Thirlwall. "You bark orders and they obey. You were kingpin and no one else mattered."

In February last year, Lisa Willis ran away from Philpott with her children, taking only the clothes they stood up in. Again, Philpott was determined he'd take possession of them, leading to the plot that killed six children. This hogwash over Philpott's benefits fudges the real issues of what went on in 18 Victory Road and in all the places Philpott set up home with unfortunate women who – as Mrs Justice Thirlwall pointed out – weren't even permitted a front door key or a bank account.

It's tiny details like this that say so much and that often only judges from diverse backgrounds can pick up on. When men like Philpott wash up in court – like he did decades ago for the double stabbing – I wish there were more women like Thirlwall to meet him and jail him for life – meaning life – the first time around.

© The Independent, 5 April 2013
www.independent.co.uk

Fred West and his wife Rosemary assaulted and murdered at least 11 women and girls, including their own children.

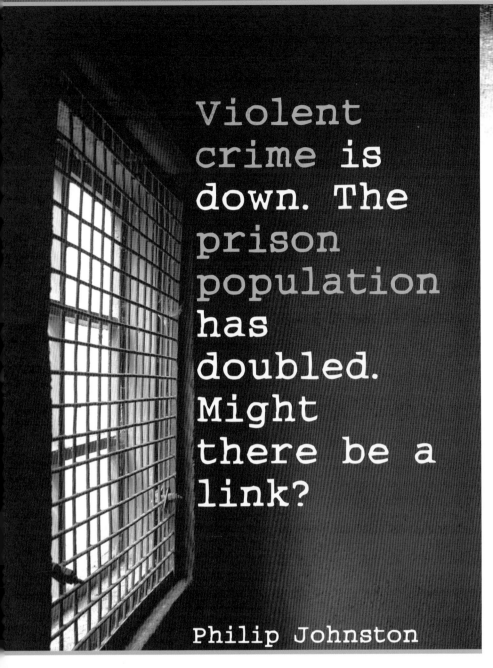

Violent crime is down. The prison population has doubled. Might there be a link?

Philip Johnston

The BBC reports a survey showing that violent crime has fallen dramatically in the UK in recent years. I must confess that I had never heard of the Institute for Economics and Peace (IEP), the organisation behind the first UK Peace Index. It appears to be linked to a global religious organisation dedicated to the promotion of world peace, and nothing wrong with that.

But the idea that Britain is now what could be called a peaceful society is wishful thinking, though it depends where you start from. For a large part of our history, extreme violence was commonplace; but the 20th century, with much higher levels of policing, saw a decline in personal violence, even as state-on-state violence grew.

Certainly, overall crime appears to have fallen over the past 20 years or so; and the new research shows violent crime has declined by about one quarter since 2003. However, crime – both violent and non-violent – remains very high compared to, say, the 1950s and 1960s, at which point it shot up both here and in the rest of the industrialised world, peaking in the mid 1990s, since when there has been a fall.

The IEP has studied police recorded crime statistics, hospital admission and treatment data and the British Crime Survey in reaching its conclusions – so the methodology seems well-founded. But what reasons can be adduced for this phenomenon?

To begin with, it will confound those who say greater inequalities in income lead to more crime since wealth differentials now are greater than they were 10 or 15 years ago. There is also an assumption that times of economic hardship lead to more crime; yet that is not true either.

The 1930s were a time of very low crime. Furthermore, since most violent crime actually involves young men attacking other young men, when they have less money they go out less – and therefore

have fewer opportunities to get drunk and have a fight. One commentator hazarded that global communication might be having a calming effect on people's behaviour.

But something else has happened since crime began to fall in the mid 1990s: the prison population has doubled. Is there a connection, and why are those poring over these statistics today seemingly reluctant to consider that there might be one? In the 1980s, the rapid rise in crime coincided with a fall in the incarceration rate and an increased use of cautions and unrecorded warnings. Studies have found strong links between the falling risk of punishment and rising crime. From 1993, Home Office policy changed and the use of prison was encouraged, especially for repeat offenders.

The last Labour government introduced a series of criminal justice laws aimed at increasing prison terms for violent offences. It is hard to believe there is no connection between the two. The problem is that there is a very powerful penal reform lobby which is determined to deny any causation: the very notion that "prison might work" is anathema to many campaigners in this field.

Even so, we still have one of the least punitive systems in Europe with fewer incarcerations per 100 offences than in many European countries. With some crimes, the incarceration rate is minuscule. In 2006, for instance, police recorded 889,000 break-ins but only 26,300 offenders were convicted. Of these, 13,350

But the idea that Britain is now what could be called a peaceful society is wishful thinking

were jailed – an imprisonment rate of 1.5 per cent.

Historically, too, you were more likely to go to jail in the past than now. In 1954, one in three robberies led to a jail sentence; today, the ratio is about one in 22. For burglaries, the differential is even more pronounced with 1 in 18 in 1954 compared with one in 59 now. If England imprisoned the same ratio of people today that it did 50 years ago, there would be around 300,000 people in prison.

A similar debate has been had in America, where violent crime has fallen far more dramatically than in the UK. Sociologists have come up with all sorts of theories, ranging from a reduction of lead in petrol affecting the behaviour of young men to the legalisation of abortion.

But in America, too, there is another constant factor: the

imposition of much harsher prison sentences since the 1980s has kept large numbers of criminals off the streets. The US incarcerates four times as many people as it did 20 years ago and the crime rate has fallen commensurately. In fact, imprisonment rates and sentence lengths are much higher in America than in the UK, which might also explain why burglary, robbery and car thefts are also lower in the US. On the other hand, Canada has experienced roughly the same decline in crime without the same lengthening of prison sentences.

It may be difficult to prove that higher prison rates cut crime but it is odd that so few people are prepared to discuss the possibility – and will reach for any explanation rather than the one staring them in the face.

The Daily Telegraph, 24 April 2013
© Telegraph Media Group Limited 2013

it's a cuddly idea: give an ex-offender a hand

but unless we reinvent our hopeless prison system that perpetuates crime, it will never work

John Bird

John Bird is founder of the Big Issue and author of The Necessity of Poverty

SOME ISSUES:

Do you think prison is the best punishment for offenders?

Should offenders just be punished, or also helped to reform?

How would you think it best to help criminals to reform and re-build a better life for themselves?

See also:

Violent crime is down... p150

Selected from Complete Issues:
No stopping them
Fact File 2013 p135

Being let out into a cold, hard world with a pittance of £46 in your back pocket and an appointment with your parole officer is not conducive to keeping a newly released prisoner on the straight and narrow.

I know because I've been there myself. It was inevitable that the first thing I would do, as a young man just released from jail, would be to find some money. I had no skills, qualifications or legal ways of raising cash so, like any member of the criminal class, I did what I knew to make a living. I thieved. And to be honest, I would have thieved over taking a low-paid, 9-to-5 job because it is an easier way of getting money.

With reoffending rates kissing 60 per cent — and a third of prisoners homeless within the first few weeks after release — the rehabilitation plan announced yesterday makes a certain amount of sense.

From next year, the Justice Secretary wants all prisoners serving less than 12 months to be mentored. A mentor, usually an ex-offender, will make contact before the prisoner has been released and then support and encourage him on the outside. The mentors will, in this vision, meet the prisoner on his release, help him to sort out accommodation and benefits and introduce him to local businesses who might give him some work.

So no more of the swift shock of reality at the prison gates: rather, a guide will help you over the hurdles of your first encounter with the outside world. Well, who could disagree with

i have known many young men who have left prison either unchanged or hardened and changed for the worse

such helpful nudging? Who could possibly object to mentoring? It's nice and cuddly for someone to listen to your problems.

But without the reinvention of prison I'm sceptical about it making much difference. "Mentoring" will only work on those who are keen to go straight and have the skills to make a living outside the world of crime. Mentoring is unlikely to crack criminal minds, especially when our shambolic prison system does little to break the psychology of the criminal class.

There are four reasons to lock someone up. To punish and get justice for the public; to deter wrongdoers from reoffending; to transform them into a better people; and, lastly, to keep them out of circulation.

In an ideal world prison would work on all these levels. But despite the billions spent, it only keeps wrongdoers out of circulation. A governor once told me that his job was to stop his charges escaping, dying or killing anyone. As for rehabilitation, that was a task that he could not get round to.

I have known many young men who have left prison either unchanged or hardened and changed for the worse. They have been biding their time, waiting to get out and carry on where they left off. And at times they have picked up new skills that are useful in the life of an opportunist criminal.

A prison system that worked would be very different from today's warehouses for criminals. It would offer an incredibly tough, disciplined regime. Everyone would have to work and learn practical skills. Prisoners would be paid for work, and have a chance to save money.

It would be expensive to run. It would also acknowledge the harsh reality that the people inside it are marked for failure by society even before they have done wrong — that crime and wrongdoing in some ways is the inevitable outcome of their circumstances. Up to 85 per cent of those in some prisons are from the jobless world of benefits dependency. Illiteracy

is high and self-esteem low. Autism, dyslexia and Asperger's are way above the national average.

I would like mentoring to work. But this scheme is like going into hospital for an operation that is cancelled and you then find that they've kindly laid on a car to get you home. But without the "operation" (the transformation inside prison), we might be putting our resources in the wrong place.

The harsh reality is that you have to spend to save. In a time of stringency maybe mentoring is all we can afford. But I doubt it will stop thousands and thousands of men prepared only for crime ending up banged up again.

The Times, 21 November 2012
© John Bird

the harsh reality is that you have to spend to save.

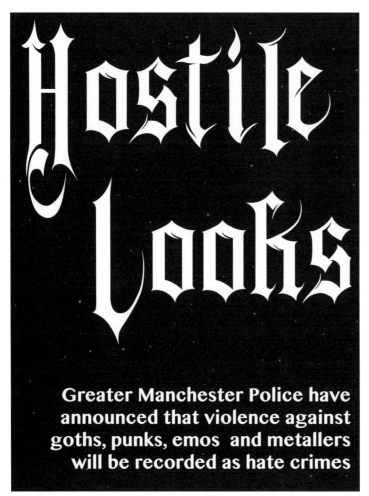

Hostile Looks

Greater Manchester Police have announced that violence against goths, punks, emos and metallers will be recorded as hate crimes

You are walking along minding your own business when the shouting begins. Taunts, insults, abuse, challenges, comments about the way you look, what you are wearing. This happens to you on most days. Sometimes it's worse. Spitting, slapping, beating, kicking. Why? Because you have piercings or pink hair or black eyeliner.

If you have been singled out as a victim because someone is prejudiced about the way you look you won't feel secure again unless that prejudice is recognised and dealt with by the forces of law. This can happen in the case of members of a religious or racial group but not, until now, in the case of those who choose to dress differently and promote alternative cultures.

In England and Wales, crimes that involve hostility or prejudice toward disability, race or ethnicity, religion or belief, sexual orientation or transgender identity are classified as hate crimes. The police record them in that way and someone convicted of a hate crime can receive an increased sentence from the court.

In April 2013 Greater Manchester Police decided to add to this list and record crimes against alternative sub-cultures as hate crimes. This means that a crime that is motivated by resentment of the way someone chooses to look or dress will be treated in the same way as other hate crime in the GMP area. The victims can expect special support and will know that the fact that they were specifically targeted has at least been recorded. The inspiration for this radical decision is the work GMP have carried out in partnership with the Sophie Lancaster Foundation.

Sophie Lancaster died in 2007 at the age of 20 after she and her boyfriend, Robert Maltby, were brutally attacked as they walked home through a park in Bacup, Lancashire. The 'reason' for the attack? Sophie and Robert were goths or 'moshers'. Sophie had piercings and dreadlocks, Robert had dyed blonde hair and eyeliner. Neither of them was dressed in extreme goth fashions but they were obviously unlike the group that attacked them.

The pair were leaving the park when Robert was hit from behind and knocked unconscious. As Sophie cradled him and tried to protect him she was brutally kicked and stamped

SOME ISSUES:

Why do 'alternative' fashions provoke hostile reactions?

Do you think the action of Greater Manchester Police will help protect alternative groups?

Will this action promote tolerance?

Should the category 'hate crime' be extended to more groups? Or is crime simply crime, no matter what the reasons behind it?

Selected from Complete Issues:
Clare's legacy
Fact File 2013 p140
Violent playgrounds
Fact File 2013 p132

on. Later the attackers would boast of having left "two moshers" "nearly dead" "a right mess".

Other teenagers in the park called the police and an ambulance. Police arriving at the scene found the pair with such severe head injuries and swelling that they could not tell which was Sophie and which was Robert. Both were in a coma and Sophie never recovered.

When her killers, who were aged between 15 and 17, were brought to trial in 2008 the prosecution argued: "Sophie and Robert were singled out not for anything they had said or done, but because they looked and dressed differently." The judge acknowledged that Sophie's killing was a hate crime because the two young people were targeted simply for being Goths.

After Sophie's death her mother, Sylvia, set up the Sophie Lancaster Foundation to leave a lasting legacy and to challenge the prejudice and intolerance towards people from alternative subcultures. Another aim, closer now to being achieved, was to have the UK Hate Crime legislation extended to include people with a different lifestyle and style of clothing.

Greater Manchester Police, in announcing their decision, noted that goths, emos, punks, metallers and members of other alternative groups have often endured abuse.

"People who wish to express their alternative sub-culture identity freely should not have to tolerate hate crime," Assistant Chief Constable Garry Shewan said.

The first time a crime was recorded as a hate crime against a sub-culture was in April 2013 when a 14-year-old boy and a 44-year-old man were charged with an assault on a teenage emo.

The scheme has not yet been adopted nationally and the courts cannot impose tougher sentences without a new law being passed. Perhaps one of the difficulties is finding a definition of a subculture – and certainly the lines between the many sub-subcultures become very blurred and indistinct to outsiders – which must include police officers.

Even the other victim, Robert Maltby, gave an interview in which he explained that although his attackers apparently had 'tribal' motives, actually:

Photo: Robert Maltby

"They just needed some kind of excuse to the beat shit out of us. I think it's more about the kind of person that attacked us. There were several attacks that summer and if you look at the kids who were responsible you could cut them all out with a cookie cutter. A guy was looking out of his window in Warrington* and saw some kids kicking his car. When he went out to stop them he was beaten to death. That happened the day before we were attacked."

Nevertheless, the GMP initiative was welcomed by many whose blatantly alternative appearance has made them the victims of daily comment, abuse and worse.

Despite the difficulties, anyone who believes in tolerance must hope that recording and, perhaps eventually punishing hate crimes based on appearance, will change attitudes towards those who, like Sophie, dare to be different. We can hope that, as the Sophie Lancaster Foundation website says, "one eight stone girl can change a generation".

Gary Newlove suffered massive head injuries and died after being beaten by a gang of youths outside his home when he confronted them about damage to a car

Source: www.sophielancasterfoundation.com and others

Religion

Christianity is part of our history so should be taught to children - it's not indoctrination.

SUSAN ELKIN

SOME ISSUES:

What parts of our culture does this writer think religion has influenced?

Why is it important to know about Christianity?

Do you need to know about Christianity even if you are not a Christian?

Do you think teachers should teach things they do not agree with?

How might this affect other lessons?

Let me set out my stall.

I am not a Christian believer. I regard most of what's in the Bible as fiction. I do not go to church and I have no religious faith of any kind.

But I live in a country which has been culturally Christian for over 1700 years. I am ethnically a Christian, whether I like it or not. Whatever I choose to believe in, Christianity as a cultural force is very much bigger than me. It has always, for example, underpinned our laws. The Reformation changed some of the details but not the principles. And we're still arguing about it. Witness the concern and anger, even from unlikely people, about the recent decision not to consecrate women.

The literature – prose, poetry and drama - which nurtures me has been deeply influenced by the various translations of the Bible and by the Book of Common Prayer for centuries. So has the music I listen to and sometimes make. If you cut all religious works out of the classical repertoire it would be a very slender version of itself without, for example all those Bach and Mozart masses amongst many other

If you cut all religious works out of the classical repertoire it would be a very slender version of itself...

A substantial amount of what you see in art galleries is rooted in Christian mythology...

They won't understand history without in-depth knowledge of Christianity either...

possible examples including the Messiah and, most of John Rutter's pieces that we hear so much of. A substantial amount of what you see in art galleries is rooted in Christian mythology too.

That's why I believe that every child in this country should learn about Christianity, its history, its tenets and its traditions. The need and right of every British child – regardless of colour and creed – to have this understanding is far more important than any individual's doctrinal squeamishness.

They won't understand history without in-depth knowledge of Christianity either. Henry VIII reformed the church so that he could marry Anne Boleyn – which must be incomprehensible to anyone who doesn't understand the complexities of the religion-led politics between Rome and the rest of the world in the 16th century and before. And how do you explain the Stuarts, the divine right of kings and the principled stubbornness of Charles I without also teaching Christianity and the different ways it has been interpreted in the past?

I have no patience with teachers who say they can't or won't teach any of this because they are atheist, agnostic or belong to another religion such as Buddhism or Islam. I don't believe in the polytheism once practised by Greeks and Romans, but it never stopped me sharing the, often very dramatic, stories of Zeus, Mercury, Aphrodite, Neptune and co with children so that they would understand the classical references in literature, art and music as well as getting a clearer idea of how those ancient peoples thought and felt.

But it doesn't happen. Or at least not enough. It was reported yesterday that an Oxford University study has found that teachers are reluctant to teach children about Christianity because they're afraid of being thought to be evangelising.

Well, don't all good teachers evangelise? I certainly used to evangelise about literature as an English teacher – and often, for that matter, about some of the magnificent language in the Bible ("with twain he covered his face, with twain he covered his feet and with twain he did fly"). The Book of Common Prayer ("the devices and desires of our own hearts") or a good traditional hymn ("slow to chide and swift to bless").

Why can't primary and specialist secondary RE teachers simply take the line: 'Just look at this idea/story/development/language. Isn't it fascinating?' You can

The need and right of every British child — regardless of colour and creed — to have this understanding is far more important than any individual's belief

Under no circumstances should we brainwash our children with religious doctrine or allow teachers to do so...

enthuse and sell all the best bits of the subject you love without trying to promote the doctrine. Information and the encouragement of interest and free thought is not, definitely not, the same as indoctrination.

At another level, there's a lot of truth in the Christian mythology just as there is in Greek and Roman myths and in any good fiction. That's why these stories have stood the test of time. It doesn't have to be literally true – that Jesus was born to a virgin in a stable for example – for there to be truth in the nativity story. It is about, for example kindness (Joseph and the inn keeper), curiosity (the shepherds), respect (the magi) and ruthless cruelty (Herod). The story says a lot about family values too. All these things I have discussed in classes with pupils, always making it clear that for me - although not for everyone - these stories are myths not reportage.

So good luck to Dr Nigel Fancourt and his colleagues on the RE programme at Oxford's Department of Education. They have just launched a series of free, new, online materials for primary and non-specialist secondary teachers to help strengthen their weak teaching about Christianity.

Under no circumstances should we brainwash our children with religious doctrine or allow teachers to do so. But we must ensure that they are knowledgeable enough about Britain's cultural religious traditions to make sense of history, politics, art, music and literature. We are failing them otherwise.

The Independent, 29 November 2012
www.independent.co.uk

...But we must ensure that they are knowledgeable enough about Britain's cultural religious traditions to make sense of history, politics, art, music and literature.

Christian news coverage is unfair

Lauren Belcher is interning at TheSite.org.

She loves travelling, campaigning against poverty, and wants to write about everything under the sun.

Lauren is fed up with the media only covering the bad bits of the Christian church, and thinks it should focus more on the good things it does too.

I'm part of the sexist, homophobic, pro-life, corrupt organisation most people call the church. Apart from, I don't think it really is all those things - not universally, anyway. I can think of dozens of amazing things Christians do, but the press only focus on the controversial issues and churn out negative headlines more frequently than Rihanna churns out albums. Why don't people get to hear the good stories? It makes me want to shout, swear, and generally behave like a very bad Christian when the media makes the church look either ridiculous or downright discriminatory.

I grew up going to church, and still go regularly. I do so not because I've been indoctrinated into a set of unfathomable and bigoted beliefs, or because I love singing 'Shine Jesus Shine'. I admit the unlimited amount of cake is a bonus, but mostly I keep going because the people are nice and so is a lot of what they think and do. Yes, some of them have dated views about women, or are against same-sex marriages, however, you'll also find a few prejudiced people if you go to your local Wetherspoons. It doesn't put me off a cheap pint, and it doesn't put me off Jesus either.

What does annoy me is that newspapers do article after article on Christians against contraception or picketing abortion clinics, and NEVER cover the positive stuff churches do. I'm part of the Church - even though I don't agree with some of the stronger opinions – because there's so much more to it. But the majority of the time you wouldn't know about the good campaigns run by churches, or the ways in which they support their local communities, because it isn't reported. Ever. What is reported is generally derogatory.

Take women bishops, for example. I doubt you missed the headlines that the synod voted against them. But did you know it was only six votes off? SIX. And would there have been as much media interest if women bishops had been voted in? I don't think so. What's not been mentioned is other churches in the UK allow women to be in all leadership roles, e.g. there've been four female presidents of the Baptist Union since the 70s. And the articles on Bristol Uni Christian Union (CU) not allowing women to be the main speaker utterly failed to mention that other CU's, like Nottingham, which had a girl president, are more supportive of women in leadership.

I'm not denying the church deserves some bad press; you can't get away from the issue of gay marriage at the moment. Admittedly, there are very few churches for it, but there are definitely Christians - myself included - who don't have a problem with it. The media paints churchgoers as homophobic imbeciles, when, in reality, most would still invite and welcome gay individuals and couples into their church.

SOME ISSUES:

What do you mainly hear about Christianity in the news?

Do you think the media should talk more about the positive things that religious organisations do?

See also:
Complete Issues
Religion

Image: IgorGolovniov/Shutterstock.com

Not every church, CU or Christian is the same, or holds the same views - but according to the headlines we all belong to the same brand of fanatical crazies.

The reality is the church does loads of good stuff! Take the work of Christian charities in international development, for example. Churches in the developing world are in a great position to know the needs of their local communities, so UK church fundraising always goes to the most useful place. We're not afraid

family who spent their free time making friends with prostitutes, addicts and the homeless. My church alone runs youth clubs, football teams, a mums and toddlers playgroup, parenting courses, a soup kitchen and regular community events. But none of this ever appears in the media.

So I know this may shock you, but not all Christians are sexist, homophobic, anti-contraception, and pro-life to the point of death. And while the press have every right to cover the bad stuff, it's only fair they mention some

Yes, some of them have dated views about women, or are against same-sex marriages, however, you'll also find a few prejudiced people if you go to your local Wetherspoons. It doesn't put me off a cheap pint, and it doesn't put me off Jesus either.

to be political either. Christian Aid campaigned for Tax Justice years before the Starbucks scandal; and Tearfund's campaigns about climate change and protecting the aid budget have swayed MPs. The church does loads in the UK too, like offering debt counselling. And despite having a judgemental reputation, I know plenty of Christians who help people most of society wouldn't spare a second for. Last week I met a

of the great things the church does, too. As for everyone else, I'm not asking that you convert, but, next time you read an article that slams the church, bear in mind the bad stuff isn't the whole story. Christians aren't all the same. We're certainly not all good, but we're not all bad - just like everyone else!

www.thesite.org, 20 December 2012

A church but no God – the atheist alternative service

It's a deliberate attempt to have the good things about attending church but without having to follow a religion or believe in God. Two comedians, Sanderson Jones and Pippa Evans, have set up 'a friendly community gathering for like-minded people' in (where else?) a former church in London.

On the first Sunday of every month The Sunday Assembly meets "to hear great talks, sing songs and generally celebrate the wonder of life. It's a service for anyone who wants to live better, help often and wonder more."

Its 'service' follows a very familiar pattern to anyone who has ever attended a church:

- Welcome / notices
- Song
- Guest speaker
- Song
- Reading
- Final Address
- Song

SOME ISSUES:

Do you agree that you can have a church without God?

Who would this assembly appeal to?

Have they focused on the best things about church or are they missing something?

What would you like to happen at the service?

Selected from Complete Issues:
First person: Graham Holter was agnostic, now he's an atheist
Essential Articles 12 p168

They even follow the church timetable, with an Easter service because: "There have been spring festivals since time began, and wouldn't it be a shame to lose 1400 years of British history over a minor theological difference? Yes. It would. Also, we love chocolate eggs!"

Their approach has more razzamatazz than Songs of Praise: "enjoy a morning that is part-foot stomping show, part-atheist church", says the website (which has not been completed because the group has been overwhelmed by interest since it was featured in national newspapers). Instead of hymns they use pop songs which everyone can join in and the sermons are on themes such as 'wonder' rather than on any scripture.

> Their approach has more razzamatazz than Songs of Praise: "enjoy a morning that is part-foot stomping show, part-atheist church"

The goal of the Assembly is "to solace worries, provoke kindness and inject a bit more whizziness into the everyday". Whizziness is not a quality associated with more conventional Sunday services.

But it's not just church services that the Assembly wants to emulate and improve on. They also want to reach out into the community, to assist and to organize volunteer groups and "try to turn good intentions into action".

So can a well-meaning group of comedians really have their cake and eat it when it comes to church services? Can they avoid the disputes and splits that plague established churches? Can they keep their congregation? It all remains to be seen. The founders are hoping that once they have a firm basis they can help others set up their own assemblies. Like any good church they want to spread the word

sundayassembly.com

Instead of hymns they use pop songs which everyone can join in and the sermons are on themes such as 'wonder' rather than on any scripture.

THE BEST BITS:
what atheists should take from religion

SOME ISSUES:

Do you have to follow a religion to have set moral codes and ideas of living?

Which of these virtues are most important and why?

What would you add to the list?

Selected from Complete Issues:
No Heaven? Why Stephen Hawking's Comment Doesn't Matter
Essential Articles 15 p160
Is there a religion for atheists?
Essential Articles 15 p162

Philosopher and writer Alain de Botton is not a believer himself but he thinks that religion has some important things to teach us.

Rather than dismissing religions, he says agnostics and atheists should instead steal from them the best ideas on how to live and organise society. Religion, he says, can give us an insight into our sense of community, relationships, emotions and more.

He suggests that in our society, being virtuous had become "a strange and depressing notion", while wickedness and evil had a "peculiar kind of glamour".

But like everything worthwhile, being good requires a bit of work. So to give his idea some structure he suggests ten key, but not easy, virtues that we should all practise.

10 virtues for atheists

1. RESILIENCE. Keeping going even when things are looking dark.

2. EMPATHY. The capacity to connect imaginatively with the sufferings and unique experiences of another person.

3. PATIENCE. We should grow calmer and more forgiving by getting more realistic about how things actually tend to go.

4. SACRIFICE. We won't ever manage to raise a family, love someone else or save the planet if we don't keep up with the art of sacrifice.

5. POLITENESS. Politeness is very linked to tolerance, the capacity to live alongside people whom one will never agree with, but at the same time, can't avoid.

6. HUMOUR. Like anger, humour springs from disappointment, but it's disappointment optimally channelled.

7. SELF-AWARENESS. To know oneself is to try not to blame others for one's troubles and moods; to have a sense of what's going on inside oneself, and what actually belongs to the world.

8. FORGIVENESS. It's recognising that living with others isn't possible without excusing errors.

9. HOPE. Pessimism isn't necessarily deep, nor optimism shallow.

10. CONFIDENCE. Confidence isn't arrogance, it's based on a constant awareness of how short life is and how little we ultimately lose from risking everything.

www.alaindebotton.com

secular britain is ruled
by religious bureaucrats

Why is the church still such a force in our society when most of us disregard its teachings?

Nick Cohen

SOME ISSUES:

Do you think a secular country should have a national religion?

Is it right that 26 bishops are given seats in the House of Lords?

Do you think religion is important in British society?

Why do people who don't practise a religion still record one on the census and other forms?

Selected from Complete Issues:
Practising Christians
Fact File 2013 p144
Believe it... or not
Fact File 2013 page 146

A few months ago, Suffolk police stopped me for driving over 30mph. My excuse that East Anglia was so flat it was impossible not to break the limit did not wash, and they sent me on a speed awareness course. Very good it was too. After surveying the human cost of bad driving, I resolved never to speed again. Unfortunately, the instructor was over-fond of his own voice and his lecture went on for hours. "I hope he winds up soon," I whispered to the woman next to me. "I am meant to be speaking to the National Secular Society."

She was a little astonished and a little amused. "A National Secular Society? Why does Britain need a National Secular Society? Surely the secularists have won?"

Falling numbers

It can feel that way. The number of people who say they have no religion jumped from 15% in the 2001 census to 25% in 2011. If the remaining 75% were believers, this leap in free-thinking would be significant but not sensational. But those who say they are religious are not faithful to their creeds, or not in any sense that the believers of the past would have recognised. Church attendance is in constant decline. Every year that passes sees congregations become smaller and greyer. As striking as the fall in religious observance is the public's near total disregard for the teachings of the clerics and prelates, who could once claim to be society's moral guides.

To cite the most striking example, a popular liberal prejudice keeps anti-Catholicism alive by picturing Catholics as automatons who blindly follow the teachings of the Vatican. There is no evidence to support it. A poll just before a papal visit in 2010 found Catholics took no more notice of the Pope than anyone else did. Just 11% of Catholics agreed with the church that doctors should perform abortions only if a woman's life was in danger. Just 4% supported Vatican teaching on contraception.

When millions of people tell the census takers they are "Christians", therefore, they are muttering the title of a childhood story they only half remember. What is more, their spiritual "leaders"

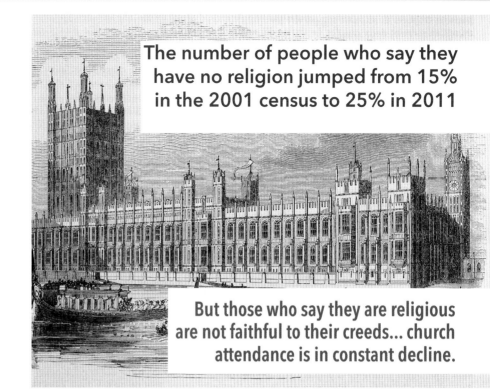

The number of people who say they have no religion jumped from 15% in the 2001 census to 25% in 2011

But those who say they are religious are not faithful to their creeds... church attendance is in constant decline.

know it. Long before the census figures were in, you could hear the screams that always accompany ideologies and institutions history is leaving behind.

The gay marriage debate

At one point in the debate about civil gay marriage, the bishops of the Church of England became so demented with fury they implied that we lived in a theocracy with clerical vetoes over democratic decision-making. "Many, within the churches and beyond, dispute the right of any government to redefine an ages-old social institution," they huffed. Meanwhile, the higher regions of the Catholic church and lower regions of the Tory party proved that they were gripped by paranoia – which, I am sure I don't need to tell you, is another classic symptom of

intellectual collapse. Joseph Devine, the Catholic bishop of Motherwell, told David Cameron that his support for gay marriage risked turning him into a modern Nero. Just in case his listeners were in any doubt that he was referring to Nero's persecution of Rome's Christians, the bishop added: "I suspect it is only a matter of time before you go one step further and outlaw the teaching of Christian doctrine on sexual morality."

A modest proposal to allow homosexual equality before the civil law – not in churches, mosques, temples and synagogues, which will remain free to enforce what tired taboos they choose – produced an immodest explosion of self-pitying rage. When you consider its impotence as well as its excess, it is easy to agree that there does not appear to be much call for secular campaigners in Britain.

Too much power?

Until you glance at how we are governed. The International Humanist and Ethical Union has just issued a grim report on the legal restrictions of freedom of thought, conscience and religion around the world. Britain has a shamefully long entry, because while everything is changing in British society, nothing is changing in the British establishment. England still has a "national" church – even though in 2010 its average weekly attendance was down to 1,116,100 (or 1.8% of the nation's population).

Twenty-six Church of England bishops are automatically granted seats in the House of Lords to support or oppose any legislation they please. On top of the decaying heap sits Elizabeth II: a grumpy priestess-queen, who in theory at least is the state religion's "supreme governor".

26 bishops sit in the House of Lords

Education

In the education system, almost one-third of state schools are run by religious authorities (and Michael Gove will ensure that number will rise). Atheist writers complain that they indoctrinate their captive audiences. I have to say that the church attendance figures, the British Social Attitudes survey and the census suggest that, if religious schools are propagandising, they are making a poor job of it.

The need for the British to enjoy equal rights to full citizenship strikes me as firmer ground for objectors to stand on. By what right do religious bureaucrats tell parents, who have paid their taxes and obeyed the law, that their children cannot attend a state-funded school because they are not devotees of the required sect? How can Britain criticise religious discrimination in other countries when it provides exemptions that allow religious schools to hire, discipline and fire teachers because the church disapproves of their beliefs or sexual orientation or marital status?

Time for change?

Challenging the growing gap between official Britain and the real Britain will not be a painless process, as the outrage over the coalition's proposals for gay marriage demonstrates. The argument for doing so with vigour is almost identical to the argument for allowing the widest possible freedom of speech. John Stuart Mill claimed in On Liberty that knowledge and self-knowledge make the individual happier – "better to be Socrates dissatisfied than a fool satisfied".

I can see no way of proving that allowing free debate proves happiness. It may well be that people are happier when their illusions and taboos remain intact. But if you prevent challenges to their beliefs, you are not treating them as adults; you are patting them on the head and saying that they cannot handle robust debates – infantilising them, in short. What applies to individuals applies to countries. Facing up to the truth about religious decline, and adapting our institutions accordingly, will doubtless cause pain to some. But it will allow Britain to become an honest and grown-up country that meets the first requirement of maturity by seeing itself as it is.

The Observer, 16 December 2012
© Guardian News & Media 2012

War & conflict

No Wonder Our Ex-soldiers Are Looking For A Fight

A new survey reveals disturbing truths about members of our armed forces

Barbara Ellen

A report in the Lancet has put together the experiences of almost 14,000 serving and former military personnel with information from the police national computer for the first time.

Links were found between active combat and post-traumatic stress disorder, alcohol abuse and depression. While overall the armed forces are less likely than civilians to offend, they are three times more likely to be convicted of violent offences; 20% of younger males (under 30) have been convicted of violence compared with 6.7% of civilians. Those who served in combat in Iraq or Afghanistan were 53% more likely to offend violently than those not on the frontline. Those with multiple experiences of combat had a 70%-80% greater risk of being convicted for acts of violence.

They were also more likely to offend before they joined up, which again made it more likely for them to be selected for combat. The report says: "Infantry units have traditionally promoted aggression as a desirable trait and such units frequently recruit individuals who are socially disadvantaged and are likely to have low educational attainment." So, let's get this straight: disadvantaged, poorly educated, young guys, who got into fights or, worse, before joining up are more likely to be sent into combat and are then more likely to be both traumatised and criminalised by their experiences. Isn't this just a modern take on "cannon fodder"?

In fairness, the military commissioned this report and says it wants to improve their care. With such statistics, there's definitely room for improvement. The report doesn't even allow for domestic violence; if it did, the figures would be even worse. One former soldier, Lewis McKay, has bravely spoken of how he felt so profoundly disturbed he found himself biting his hands to stop himself from hitting his wife. I say "bravely", because all seem agreed that one of the biggest problems is the stigma surrounding mental health issues.

"Infantry units have traditionally promoted aggression as a desirable trait and such units frequently recruit individuals who are socially disadvantaged and are likely to have low educational attainment."

Some of you might be thinking, well, it's obvious that naturally aggressive people are good choices for combat. Some might even think that maybe it's the best place for these "meat-heads". After all, if they were offending prior to joining up, then the violence would be happening anyway, just out on the streets instead of in combat. It makes sense to put these violent sorts in the military and make use of it.

What rot. Just as boy racers tend to grow out of speeding, there's more than a chance that other young men would grow out of violence. Just because someone commits violence when they are very young, it doesn't mean that they're going to be violent for ever. The goal for most young men enlisting in the forces would be learning a trade, not learning how to be better at violence.

For some, being flung into combat, sometimes repeatedly, might prolong and enhance violent tendencies they might otherwise have grown out of. The irony is that when they leave active duty, the same single-minded aggression is swiftly denounced as "wrong again" by wider society. Is it any wonder they are so messed up?

And then probably abandoned. While it's encouraging to hear that the military wants to do more, you only have to see how physically disabled soldiers are treated in this country (many forced to rely on charities) to imagine how all these good intentions are going to pan out in this era of swingeing cuts.

The irony is that when they leave active duty, the same single-minded aggression is swiftly denounced as "wrong again" by wider society. Is it any wonder they are so messed up?

There is also a disquieting ethical element to the way certain types of (troubled, disadvantaged) young males have an increased chance of ending up in direct combat – not just risking physical death and injury, but also long-term psychological damage.

This is what I mean by "cannon fodder". The dictionary definition is "soldiers regarded merely as material to be expended in war". It's supposed to be an archaic term, but, for too many, it probably doesn't seem that way.

The Observer, 17 March 2013
© Guardian News and Media Ltd 2013

The unique advantage of female war reporters in Muslim countries

Most of the first correspondents to file reports from Gaza when the latest conflict began last week were women.

Emma Barnett **discovers what their unique advantage is over their male colleagues in Muslim cities and countries.**

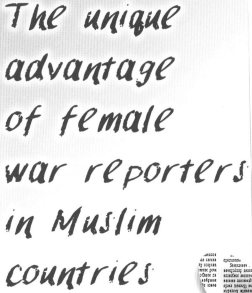

SOME ISSUES:

Why do you think women may be better suited to reporting from war situations?

What are the dangers in being a war reporter?

Why do you think people are often more concerned for the safety of female reporters than men?

Is this fair?

Selected from Complete Issues:
Snapshot
Fact File 2011 p161

Phoebe Greenwood was frantically filing her latest piece for The Telegraph in Gaza City earlier this week when she noticed something.

Sat in the main lobby of the Al Deira Hotel, which has become effectively become a big newsroom in the war-torn strip of land, Greenwood observed that all of the correspondents of the American, Australian, Spanish and British broadsheets writing around her were women.

Jodi Rudoren (New York Times), Ruth Pollard (Sydney Morning Herald), Harriet Sherwood (Guardian), Ana Carbajosa (El Pais), Abeer Ayyoub (freelance Palestinian journalist) and Rolla Scolari (Sky Italia) have all been Greenwood's comrades during the latest troubles in the Middle East. On the job she has also been accompanied by Heidi Levine, whom she describes as a "ridiculously tough war photographer" and worked alongside Eman Mohammed Darkhalil, an award-winning and heavily pregnant photographer.

At the start of the latest Israel-Gaza conflict last week, Greenwood, a freelance reporter based in Jaffa, Tel Aviv, said the majority of the correspondents first on the ground were women and what's even better, it's no longer remarkable.

"I think this high number of female correspondents in a conflict zone is as a result of gender-equality finally filtering down – making it totally normal for women to report from the front line," she explains.

"Obviously there were the superstars who paved the way such as Kate Adie, Marie Colvin and Orla Guerin but now we are on a total equal footing to the men when it comes to reporting in conflict zones."

This reality couldn't have been more clearly on show than during the Libyan revolution last year – when the first three reporters into Green Square, Tripoli, were all women: Alex Crawford of Sky News, Sara Sidner, of CNN, and Zeina Khodr, of al-Jazeera English.

A bomb going off on US soil is a rarity

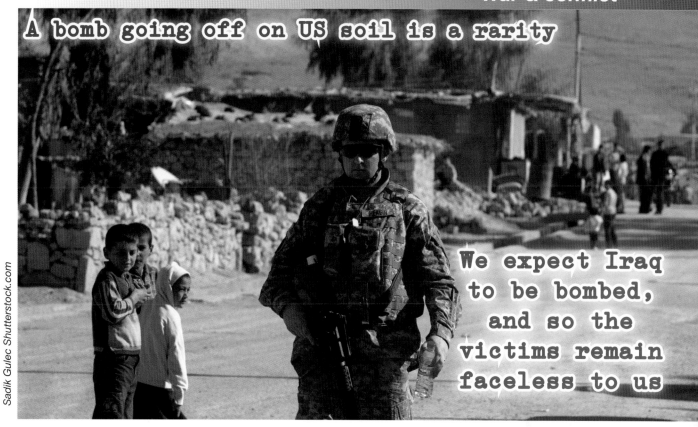

Sadik Gulec Shutterstock.com

We expect Iraq to be bombed, and so the victims remain faceless to us

But it was a subsequent tweet that provoked uproar among some. It was drawn to my attention that, the same day, a succession of car bombs had murdered large numbers of Iraqis. And so I added: "Thoughts with the people of Iraq, too. At least 31 dead in yet another day of bombs. Horrific." A tirade of abuse – admittedly from a minority – followed: stripping the venom away, the essential argument was that such a tweet was a political statement, attempting to water down the significance of the Boston bombing by putting it in a context of far greater bloodshed elsewhere. We should not be focusing on the dead and maimed in Boston, because such nightmares are a daily occurrence elsewhere and are yet ignored – or so my tweets were interpreted.

Shamefully, I defended myself by pointing out that I had tweeted about Boston first. Why would I do that,

asked other detractors. We are all made of flesh and bone; we are all humans who have fears, aspirations and insecurities. We all fall in love, have dreams we'd like to realise, do things we regret. Why is the slaughter of innocent people in Boston any more shocking or newsworthy than the deaths of Arabs?

The former editor of the Mirror, Roy Greenslade, calls this the "hierarchy of death". Referring to Northern Ireland Troubles, he wrote of how "in the first rank – getting the most prominent coverage – are British people killed in Britain; in the second, the security forces, whether army or RUC; in the third, civilian victims of republicans; and, in the fourth, garnering very little coverage indeed, the victims of loyalists." In other words, newspaper editors made a judgement on the newsworthiness of blood being spilled based on the perceived value of the lives lost.

It's wrong to simply blame newspaper editors, of course. If we are all to be honest with ourselves, our level of shock and distress at death is often tempered by various factors. "Cultural proximity" is certainly one. American cities seem familiar to us; we share a language; the way their citizens live their lives seem similar to our own, allowing us to empathise more easily. The way Iraqis live may seem difficult to comprehend, almost another world to many of us. And then there is the sense of what is normal. A bomb going off on US soil is certainly a rarity indeed; thousands of bombs – whether hidden in cars or dropped from aeroplanes – have detonated in Iraq over the last decade. We expect Iraq to be bombed, and so the victims remain faceless to us; the emotional impact of thousands of deaths – for most – is almost nil.

This hierarchy of death emerges in other conflicts, too. A study of Associated

Many young black men die violently with little media coverage

Photo: fmual/Shutterstock.com

It was affluent, young, pretty white women suffering harm who were the most likely to provoke a media frenzy. Madeleine McCann is, of course, one of the most famous missing little girls of our times. Would she have received the same level of attention if her parents were a working-class couple – and black or Asian, for example?

Much of this may seem like stating the obvious, and that is disturbing in itself: it suggests that we are almost resigned to what is treated as a mere fact of life. But placing human suffering into hierarchies allows injustices to continue without scrutiny or challenge; and it distorts our understanding of the reality of conflicts. It undermines a universal, shared sense of humanity. It is, ultimately, a manifestation of prejudice.

So no – to answer my Twitter detractors – I do not believe the unbearable horrors that take place on a daily basis mean the anguish of Boston is somehow irrelevant. But all of us have a responsibility to challenge our own prejudices, and to work on empathising with fellow humans who suffer in lands distant – in miles or culture – from our own. Failing to empathise with suffering allows us to tolerate it; and, in doing so, we become complicit in its existence.

© The Independent, 21 April 2013
www.independent.co.uk

Press reports on the Israel-Palestine conflict found that Israeli deaths were covered at twice the rate of those of Palestinians. Or take the Democratic Republic of Congo, the site of the bloodiest conflict since the Second World War. It is estimated that over five million people have perished since the late 1990s, and yet it has barely punctured public consciousness. Yet conflicts in the Balkans – dreadful on their own terms, but significantly less bloody – dominated headlines throughout the 1990s. It undoubtedly had much to do with the fact the victims there were Europeans.

It would be reassuring to claim that those who die closer to us – for example, in the community in which we live – will provoke the greatest emotional impact – it hits home harder. But many young black men die violently with little media coverage; there are many explanations, many of them deeply uncomfortable.

Sheri Parks, a professor of American studies at the University of Maryland, has coined the term "Missing White Woman Syndrome", arguing that the deaths of black women – and particularly black men – were often ignored in comparison.

Wider world

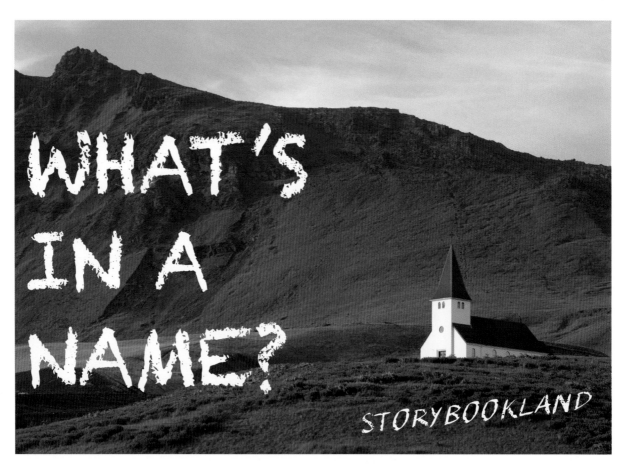

WHAT'S IN A NAME?

STORYBOOKLAND

An advertising campaign to boost tourism wanted you to consider Iceland – by another name

SOME ISSUES:

What do you think of the idea of re-naming a country?

How important is a name for a country, a town or a person?

Selected from Complete Issues:
The name game
Essential Articles 13 p138

What do you picture when someone mentions Iceland? I mean the country, not the shop. What do you picture? Ice.

You may remember the volcano with the unpronounceable name (Eyjafjallajökull) that caused all the trouble with air traffic in 2010 – but I bet you picture it covered in ice. Lakes, geysers, mountains, rivers, sea, coast – you imagine them all covered in or surrounded by ice.

And that's a problem for Iceland's tourist board. This is the most sparsely populated country in Europe and its two main industries – fishing and finance – have struggled. A boost to its tourism would be warmly welcomed, but the very name of the country is a handicap in marketing its delights. So the tourist board has launched a competition to re-name the country, removing the 'ice' part that was putting people off.

On the website, *Inspired by Iceland*, visitors were invited to enter a competition to find the best new name.

Some contributors seemed to miss the point or see no real need for change. The person who suggested it should be called "Snowy Swissland" felt "Ice is fine". The suggestion "Uberfrostyland" wouldn't tempt many nor would "Rainland", "Sometimessnowland" or even "Winterwonderland" or "Toasty Sweaterland".

For others the non-ice-related parts of the scenery were the inspiration for rather literal names: Volcano Land, Sea Land, Green and Blue Land. At least the suggestions Aurora Land and Hot Water Land were relating to a special quality of the country, as was the frequent suggestion "Fire and Ice Land". More inspiring, perhaps, were the responses to that scenery "Spectacular-", "Unique-" "Extreme-" lands were offered

A whole group of people saw the country as mystical and other-worldly. There were many suggestions of "Dreamland", "Neverland", "Wonderland", "Fairyland", "Storybook Land". For some it was the unearthly quality of the place: "Moonland" and "Anotherplaneticeland" were suggested.

Some entries were never going to win the competition. If "Unicornland" had been chosen, surely tourists would have been berating the authorities for misrepresentation. While "Cleanupafterdogland" inspired, according to the proposer by seeing "many dog owners who cared for their pets as much as they care for the cleanliness of their streets", seems unlikely to bring tourists by the bus load.

The country had clearly captured the hearts of many, in fact "Heartland" was a popular suggestion. Others called it their "True Homeland", "Heartchosenland" and "Lovetouchedland".

For others the defining quality of Iceland was the sense of space and freedom both literally – "BreatheFreeLand" – and in the tolerance of its society. "There is freedom to be who you really are here, to live like someone left the gate open!!! ..." explains someone whose competition entry name is "Nice land".

So was the tourist board successful? Well if you've read this far you'll know that, far from being just ice, Iceland is a magical place, unlike any other on earth with wonderful colours, and extreme scenery. It's a place that people love and warm to, where they can feel free to be themselves. OK, so it doesn't have unicorns but it does have considerate people who don't leave dog mess lying around.

And who is telling you this? Not the tourist board who obviously have a sales pitch, but other ordinary people who have been to Iceland and love it. You would have to commend the tourist board on having run a brilliant campaign.

And what won the prize of a trip to Iceland? As the website says: "the beautiful landscapes and magical nature really caught your imagination, making Isle of Awe Land the world's favourite name for Iceland!"

Sources: Various
www.inspiredbyiceland.com

DELHI GANG RAPE VICTIM'S TRAGIC DEATH TRANSFORMS HER FAMILY'S LIFE

In December 2012, a 23 year old woman and a male friend went to watch a film at a shopping centre. On their way home they boarded a bus which turned out to have been commandeered by a group of men. These men raped and tortured the woman and beat her friend with iron rods. The two were stripped, robbed and dumped on the roadside near the city's main airport. The woman had been so seriously assaulted that she lost most of her intestines. She died from her injuries on 29th December.

BY JASON BURKE

SOME ISSUES:

Do you think the new life for the family is any compensation for their loss?

Do you agree that the situation for women seems worse in India than in other countries?

How could people change deep-rooted attitudes?

See also:
Complete Issues
Rape

THE VICTIM'S FATHER RECALLS HER AMBITIONS AND FINAL DAYS JUST AS FAMILY HOPES OF A BETTER LIFE FINALLY ARRIVE – AT THE HIGHEST COST

Soon the narrow lane with dirt floor that leads through the leaning tenements and market stalls will be a distant memory. So too will the evening ritual of spreading out a plastic sheet over a bed to turn it into a dining table. Food will no longer be prepared in a tiny kitchen crammed with spotless tin utensils. The four toothbrushes – once five – will no longer be stored in a battered plastic holder outside the washroom.

Thousands of families move to better accommodation every day in Delhi. A marginally lesser number slip into greater poverty. And so India moves, incrementally but seemingly ineluctably, towards prosperity.

But the move that will take these two young men and their parents from a two-room basement to a spacious "middle-income" government-built apartment with running water and continuous power is far from ordinary. Nor has it much to do with a new "India Shining". The new home is a gift from the local authorities and, in the cold language of bureaucrats, described as "compensation" for the death of the young woman, their daughter and sister, who died of injuries sustained during a brutal gang rape by six men three months ago this week.

The incident prompted a global outcry, weeks of protests in India and calls for a wide-ranging legal and policing reform. It led to a fierce debate on the wave of sexual violence to women in India and the social attitudes that some say are responsible.

On Monday, the principal accused in the rape case, Ram Singh, 33, was found hanged in Delhi's Tihar prison. An inquiry has been launched into what India's minister for home affairs admitted was a "serious security lapse". The victim's eldest brother, 20, said the family was disappointed the man had been able to chose the time of his own death.

Singh was on trial with five others at a specially established fast-track court in Delhi and faced the death sentence.

In an interview with the Guardian, the 23-year-old victim's father remembered the moment when a policeman rang him, at about 10pm on a cold December evening, to tell him there had been an "accident" and that he would find his daughter at a hospital 10 miles across the city from his home in the scruffy outlying suburb of Dwarka.

A friend with a motorbike took him through Delhi's busy traffic. "She was lying on a stretcher, covered by a green blanket," he said. The family have not been identified in the Indian press due to strict local laws.

"I thought she was unconscious but when I laid my hand on her

Bangladeshi girls hold placards as they stand to form a human chain to protest against the recent gang rape

Photo: AP Photo/A.M. Ahad

forehead she opened her eyes. She was crying. I told her: 'It'll be alright, beta [child]'."

Hours later came bad news.

"I was waiting outside the operating theatre. A doctor came out. He said she would probably not last more than a few hours, certainly more than a day or so," the father said.

But the girl held on much longer, twice giving a crucial statement to investigators. On 25 December, she closed her eyes for the last time.

"During the evening, maybe 9pm, she saw me standing outside the intensive care unit.

"She turned to look at me and gestured for me to come. She asked me if I had eaten. I said yes. Then she said: 'Dad, go to sleep, you must be tired.' I patted her head. She said: 'You should get some sleep.'

"She took my hand and kissed it. That moment hurts me more every time I think about it. She never opened her eyes again."

His daughter died days later, in a clinic in Singapore where she and the family had been flown by the Indian government for specialised treatment.

Unlike many parents in India, where sons are usually favoured, the family had spared nothing for their daughter.

A first son had died days after being born and the new child was so welcome "we did not care if it was a boy or a girl as long as it survived," the father said.

She was born in Delhi. Her father had moved to the city from his village in a remote part of the poor, lawless northern state of Uttar Pradesh. He left, reluctantly, his patch of inherited land too small to provide for a family. "I had no choice. I had to move to the city to have a chance of a better life," he said.

He worked in factories and, in recent years, as a loader at Delhi's domestic airport, working double eight-hour shifts unloading planes from places he could never visit to bring home 200 rupees (£2.50) every day.

With no savings, he sold part of his land and mortgaged the rest to raise the 45,000 rupees (£600) annual fee for his daughter's training as a physiotherapist at a college in the northern city of Dehradun.

The young woman worked in call centres to cover the 50,000 rupees (£660) living expenses. The family hoped that her earnings would eventually be enough to pay for the college fees of her two younger brothers and perhaps a better life.

In their small home, stifling in the 45C heat of the Delhi summer, freezing in the chill winters, the young woman had a bedroom to herself, to sleep and, above all, to study.

The rest of the family slept next door in the only other room. She covered a wall in notes and posters – not of Bollywood stars as many Indian teenagers would have done – but of formulae and diagrams culled from her science text books.

"I read somewhere that pulling yourself out of

Women-only subway car, Delhi

Photo: joyfull/Shutterstock.com

poverty means working like a horse and living like a saint. That is what I have always done. That is what my children have been taught to do. That is what my daughter did," her father said.

In death, she has transformed her family's life. Not only are they moving to a new home, of a size and standard they could never have been able to afford, but three separate state governments have made payments worth £50,000. Previously, the family's entire savings never amounted to more than the equivalent of £100. Her 18-year-old brother has been given a coveted job in a subsidiary of Indian railways.

The family have not been attending the trial.

"What would I do if I saw them? I'd want to kill them but I am helpless," the father said.

The men are now facing the death penalty for the assault that took place in a moving bus and the brother said on Monday the suicide of the alleged ringleader should change nothing. A juvenile also detained for his role in the attack should be hanged, too, he added.

"I have faith in the government. Every citizen should trust the government of his country to see that justice is done," the father explained.

He and his wife chose their new home close to where they have lived for decades and where their children grew up. Only a few days ago, they packed her clothes and books away.

"I console myself that she was a good soul, set free in death," he said.

The Guardian, 12 March 2013
© Guardian News and Media Ltd 2013

This case provoked huge protests inside and outside India as well as a critical examination of cultural attitudes to women because although this was an extreme and shocking example it was far from being unique. Protesting women spoke of constant harassment by individual men and by groups and there is plenty of evidence that sexual violence is seen as normal.

For example, in July 2012, news channels showed video footage of a teenage girl being sexually assaulted by a laughing mob of more than 12 men in a busy street outside a bar in north-east India. No one intervened for up to 45 minutes.

In an incident in Mumbai, a 24-year-old man was stabbed to death when he rebuked men who were harassing a female friend. His cousin said later, "If you try and stop harassment on a train or in the street then you are the one who people get angry at."

In 1966 Indira Gandhi made history as the country's first female prime minister, yet a global poll in 2012 voted India the worst G20 country for women, behind

even Saudi Arabia. One reason was the high rate of female infanticide, with sons being valued so much more than daughters female foetuses are often aborted and female babies left to die. Other reasons include child marriage and slavery.

"In India, women and girls continue to be sold as chattels, married off as young as 10, burned alive as a result of dowry-related disputes and young girls exploited and abused as domestic slave labour," said Gulshun Rehman, of Save the Children UK.

Within such an atmosphere, people hoping for a change in attitudes have a desperate fight on their hands.

As Samar Halarnkar wrote in the Hindustan Times, India is "no country for women...we, Indian men, set unwritten limits for our women, and if they do not stay within those limits, we perpetrate the worst abuses against them. Men abuse women in every society, but few males do it with as much impunity, violence and regularity as the Indian male."

In Saudi Arabia, women are confined by technology

Minky Worden

Text messages are the ultimate convenience, used by people worldwide to communicate, often to notify friends and families of their whereabouts. In many countries, new technologies can serve to enhance individual liberty. But technology does not always liberate.

Last month, the kingdom of Saudi Arabia expanded a system in which it sends Saudi men text messages, known as SMS, to notify them when their wives or other "dependents" leave the country, as part of its regulations requiring women to obtain permission from their guardians to travel. In a twist that proves technology's power, Manal al-Sharif, the woman who in 2010 launched a campaign to obtain for women the right to drive, used Twitter to inform the world of the story.

In Saudi Arabia, women are treated as legal minors, no matter how old they are. Saudi women can't study, drive or make education decisions for themselves or their children without the permission of a male "guardian" – a father, husband, brother or son. Millions of schoolgirls are barred from playing sports. Unemployment among Saudi women who want to work is 34 percent, and women who have advanced degrees struggle to find employment in the segregated society. Women need a guardian's permission even for some medical treatments.

In recent years, the Saudi government has adopted some initiatives to enhance women's participation in public life. In 2011 Saudi authorities granted women the right to obtain licenses to practice law. Women are now allowed to represent clients in court and to open law firms under their own names. This past summer, the kingdom allowed two women to compete in the London Olympics - the first time female athletes had ever represented Saudi Arabia at the Games.

SOME ISSUES:

Why do you think women are treated in this way in Saudi Arabia?

Do you think the government has the right to enforce such conditions?

Should anyone intervene to improve the state of women there?

Selected from Complete Issues:
Women's rights are human rights
Essential Articles 12 p190
A war against women
Essential Articles 13 p194

But the government continues to deny more than half of its people the right to make decisions about the most important aspects of their lives. As long as this system remains in place, women will remain unable to secure an equal role in Saudi society.

The government is broadening the SMS notification program as a technological advance over "yellow slips," the paperwork Saudi women were for years required to present when travelling internationally to prove that their male guardians allowed the trip.

In a 2008 report, "Perpetual Minors," Human Rights Watch told the story of Fatma A., a 40-year-old woman living in Riyadh who could not board a plane without her "yellow slip." After she was divorced, Saudi authorities had transferred her guardianship to her son because her father was dead. "My son is 23 years old

and has to come all the way from the Eastern Province to give me permission to leave the country," she said.

In the newspaper Al-Sharq last month, Brigadier Abdullah Abdel Kader described the SMS notification as a technological advance to ease travel. "Saudi Arabia plans to implement more e-services in the future," he said. "Ninety-five percent of people who go through King Fahd Airport now use it. It's a positive thing that people are signing up because the aim of the system is to facilitate the ability of people to exit the country."

The yellow-slip system was both discriminatory and cumbersome. But all the text-message system does is to use modern technology to enforce a retrograde double standard that denies women control over their own travel.

A tiny bright spot in this sad situation is that Internet-based communication is also giving a

It is jarring to see a government use the latest digital technology to enforce medieval treatment of women

voice to Saudi women to demand equal treatment. Manal al-Sharif pointed out this month that "the small fact of the SMS story gives you the idea of the bigger problem with the whole guardianship system."

It is jarring to see a government use the latest digital technology to enforce medieval treatment of women. One hopes at least that digital technology can increasingly give voice to courageous women fighting for equality, and for their supporters outside Saudi Arabia to press for structural reform of the kingdom's backward policies.

Minky Worden is director of global initiatives for Human Rights Watch and editor of The Unfinished Revolution, a book on women's rights around the world.

Source: Human Rights Watch
www.hrw.org

The King Khaled Foundation, a Saudi Arabian charity, has begun its first ever ad campaign against domestic violence, using an image of a woman with a bruised left eye behind her niqab.

The text says:

'Some things can't be covered'

In Saudi Arabia, women are classed as wards of their husbands or fathers and need permission from a male guardian to travel, work, marry, study – or even open a bank account.

They must wear traditional Islamic dress outside the home.

There are no laws to protect victims of domestic abuse and rape victims can find themselves accused of adultery.

In a culture where 53% of men admitted to sometimes hitting their wives, this ad campaign is seen as shocking and powerful.

A typical day in the life of an Internally Displaced Person in Mali

By Muganzi M. Isharaza

It is 5am in a small town in central Mali. The sun, while not yet visible, has already started casting away the dark cold night. And in a tiny two-roomed house, hardly larger than twelve square metres, Miriam, age 32, awakes. She walks around the children who stir in their sleep, careful not to step on or wake them. Altogether, there are nine children squeezed in one room, while the second room acts as a pantry and "living room," though there's hardly any space for them to sit. With only one room to sleep in, they are still among the lucky ones: compared with many other internally displaced persons (IDPs), having all her children with her, in one tiny space, is actually a luxury.

"Some of the other families that fled Timbuktu had no choice but to leave their adult children there to take care of the land and property," she says, "and now, every night they worry about whether or not their children are alive."

This worry has not stopped for the Touareg families like Miriam's who fled into Central Mali from Timbuktu and other places in the North. Touaregs are light skinned Malians and have traditionally lived in the Northern part of the country. However, because the anti-Government militants in this region are often of a similar light complexion, many other Malians believe that all Touaregs support the armed opposition groups who imposed vicious laws on the

SOME ISSUES:

Would you be happy to take in relatives who were displaced?

Would your relatives be happy to help you in the same circumstances?

What do you imagine the future holds for Miriam and for her children?

Selected from Complete Issues:
Forced to flee
*Fact File 2012 p158
(see also Fact File 2014 for statistics on Internally Displaced Persons)*

> **There are nine children squeezed in one room, while the second room acts as a pantry and "living room"**

Young displaced girls eat food provided by charities

Photo: UNHCR/H. Gaux, November 2012

fabled Northern Malian city before the French troops came. Because of this, revenge attacks against Touaregs and even killings have been reported in several parts of the country.

Miriam prepares breakfast for her children, before waking them up at 6:30, prepares them for school and at 7, serves their breakfast and sends them off. She then sweeps the yard, tidies up the two rooms she now calls home and then heads to the market.

"The market here is not very different from the one back home," she says, "but I can afford far less than I used to."

Miriam, fled Timbuktu with her children on January 9th, but her husband, Yussuf, had insisted on staying there to take care of the family's property; as of 30th January, she had yet to hear from him and does not know whether he has survived. She's heard of the successful recapture of Timbuktu by the Malian and French armies, but that does little to settle her mind.

Like most internally displaced people in Mali, Miriam has moved in with relatives and relies on them for her livelihood. She is living in a small corner of their house, eating their food and even wearing their clothing. It is they who are taking care of her, now that she's separated from her husband and has no income of her own.

"All day and all night, all I worry about is him. I worry that he is dead. Then I tell myself not to think of such horrible things," she says, before adding, "But then, I really can't help it. He's on my mind all the time."

There's also not enough food to go around.

"Because I came with the children, there is not enough

Like most internally displaced people in Mali, Miriam has moved in with relatives and relies on them for her livelihood

Asa Askofari, 24, fled Northern Mali in April 2012 with her husband and family

Photo: UNHCR/G. Gordon, January 2013

food to go around," she explains. "We therefore decided that the adults get only breakfast and lunch and the children share for supper whatever food is leftover from lunch."

Things were not always this way. In Timbuktu, Miriam – a teacher by profession – had a job at a primary school. Her husband was a trader of livestock and jewellery. They had a few livestock and a small backyard vegetable garden. In Timbuktu, they could afford three meals a day for everyone. They weren't rich, but at least they could afford to feed their family.

"Here, I feel like I am a burden to my parents. It is because of me and the children that they now have to eat two

meals instead of three," she laments, "Of course they do not complain about it, but it is still the fact."

At noon, the school-going children come running home. They quickly eat their food and rush to play. For most of the afternoon, Miriam sits on the verandah of her tiny quarters, sipping tea and thinking about better days.

"Each time I look at the children, I know I smile, knowing that at least they are safe," she says, "But each time they get out of my sight, my thoughts go back to home and my husband."

Miriam doesn't know what will happen in the next few weeks. While the armed opposition groups have fled Timbuktu, revenge killings are still being reported and she has yet to hear from her husband. If he's alive, she and the children may consider returning home in the next month or so when things have settled down. Otherwise... well, Miriam doesn't want to think of the alternatives. And yet, for now until an uncertain time in the future, it's all she can do.

Source: World Vision, 5 February 2013
www.worldvision.org.uk

"I feel like I am a burden to my parents"

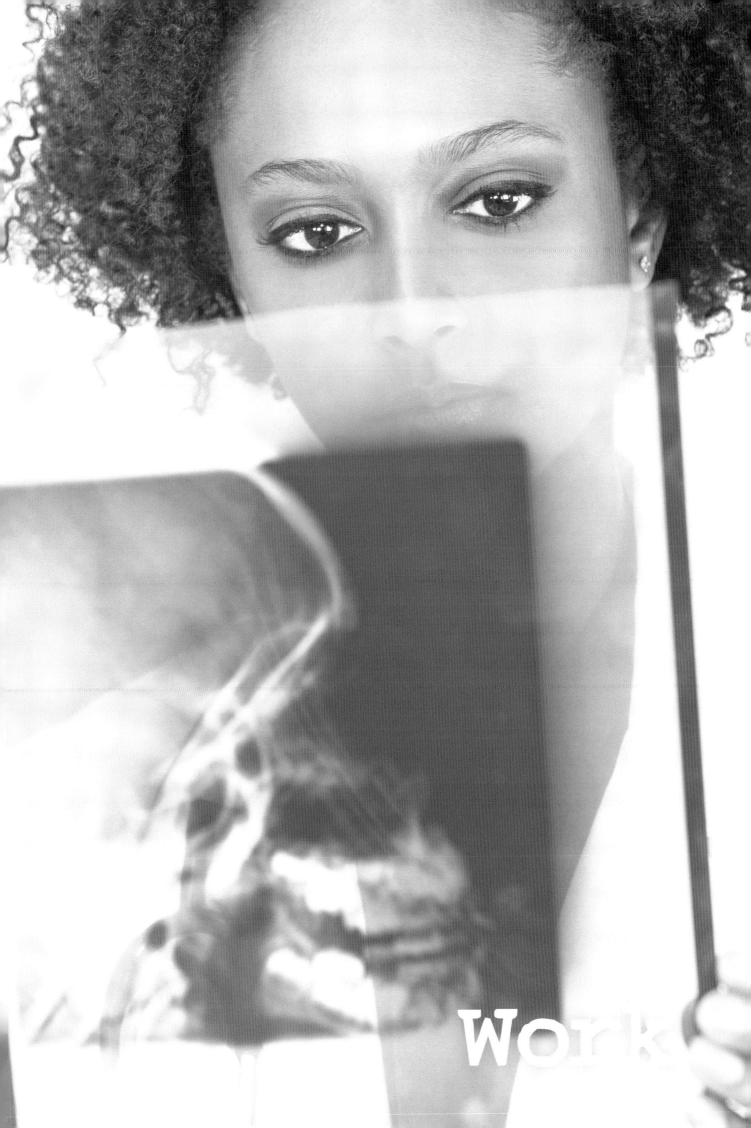

You need a job. But are you shouting loud enough?

(Like Adam Pacitti, who used a billboard)

Today's graduates emerge from uni into a hostile job market and they're willing to do whatever it takes. That's bad news for those of us who have to watch.

ALICE JONES

SOME ISSUES:

Do you think this is a good way of getting yourself a job?

Why do you think graduates are struggling to get work?

What ideas do you have about how to find work?

What would you do if you were down to your last £500, unemployed and staring a lifetime in the dole queue in the face? Stockpile baked beans and other non-perishables? Invest half in an ISA and feel financially savvy but really poor for a year? Or perhaps buy 500 scratchcards and hope for the best?

Don't be daft. You'd rent a billboard, of course. That's what Adam Pacitti has done. The 24-year-old, who graduated from Winchester University with a first-class degree in media production, can't get a job. Or, more specifically, can't get a job he actually wants. So he has spent the last £500 of his savings on a billboard in Shoreditch, a part of east London dubbed "Silicon Roundabout" by its many new-media denizens, and Old Street roundabout by everyone else.

"I spent my last £500 on this billboard. Please give me a job. Employadam.com" runs the giant advert, accompanied by a picture of Pacitti wearing the start-up upstart uniform of heavy-rimmed specs and floral shirt. The link leads to a video CV, in which Pacitti speaks of his desire to get a job in film production, broadcasting, advertising or any job in the "ultra-competitive, cut-throat and slightly vacuous industry that is the media".

It's all quite tongue-in-cheek, a bid for attention or perhaps a pitch for a brief career as a panel-show guest as much as for a first-round interview. But in an industry where limelight-grabbing and self-promotion are key workplace skills, going viral could be a wise career move. It's probably a lot more fun (if rather costlier) than typing out a boring old CV, trying to remember what grade you got in GCSE biology, bigging up your Duke of Edinburgh bronze award and extracting "transferable skills" from a brief stint as a glass-washer at a Wetherspoon.

So good luck to Adam. He needs it. Today's graduates emerge from university, clutching their scrolls, into a hostile world. About 40 per cent of university-leavers fail to get a graduate job more

It's all quite tongue-in-cheek, a bid for attention or perhaps a pitch for a brief career as a panel-show guest as much as for a first-round interview.

than two years after leaving education. There are close to a million 18- to 24-year-olds out of work. Students who began their courses in September 2012 can look forward to leaving in June 2015 with up to £27,000 in debts. As a result, more and more young people do not believe a degree is worth the paper it is printed on: this year the numbers applying to university fell for a second consecutive year, by 6.8 per cent, and are now at their lowest since 2009. In the

jungle of the job market, it is every man for himself.

Is the billboard, then, the shape of things to come? Certainly, shouting about one's unemployed status in public is characteristic of an era of self-splurging and oversharing instigated by Facebook and Twitter. In future, will graduates have to come up with ever wackier ways to sell, sell, sell their personalities, applying for jobs in the manner of desperate reality television hopefuls, because

personality and infamy count for more than skills and experience? It doesn't bear thinking about.

At the time of writing, Pacitti was still jobless. "I haven't had any firm offers yet, but there's been a lot of support," he said. I hope it works out for him, but if he's still unemployed this time next year, I'm sure Celebrity Big Brother would be delighted to have him.

© The Independent, 4 January 2013
www.independent.co.uk
Photos: www.employadam.com

Success

Adam received around sixty solid job offers after launching the Employ Adam campaign. At the time of going to press he had taken a job with KEO Digital as a viral producer for projects including River Cottage, Crowdfunder and Hugh's Fish Fight. To show his gratitude to everyone who shared his website he hired a billboard.

Can a four day working week actually work?

The bible says the world was created in seven days, the Beatles sang about eight days a week – but it is a four day working week that many Britons want

In recent years our living and working patterns have changed and are still changing. Sunday shopping, internet shopping, mobile technology, flexitime and working from home all make a pattern of five days of work with two days of rest less of a natural one. Yet rather than working to suit the service-based economy we now live in, the majority of us still have work patterns based on the manufacturing life of the last century: the conventional 8 hour day, five day week, with commuting time on top.

But many Britons would like to change this, preferring to lengthen their working day by an extra two hours in order to gain a whole extra day off at the weekend. 72% opted for exactly that in a YouGov poll in February 2013.

This pattern, known as 4/10 (four days of ten hours), has obvious advantages - a three-day weekend being the great attraction. Those in favour say that employees return to work refreshed, ready and more productive. Firms save on heating and lighting by closing for an extra day. Transport costs are reduced, one day's worth of commuting time is saved and the environment benefits!

SOME ISSUES:

Do you think a four day working week is a better idea?

How would it affect education and learning?

What do you think would be the positives and negatives of a four day working week?

Selected from Complete Issues:
Who's busiest?
Fact File 2012 p190

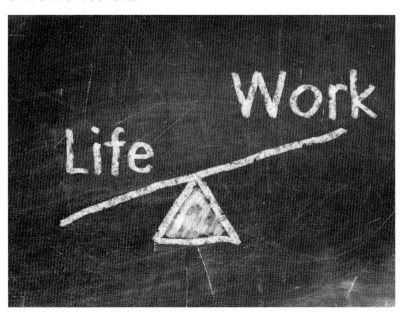

Firms save on heating and lighting by closing for an extra day. Transport costs are reduced, one day's worth of commuting time is saved

One person who is convinced of the advantages is President Yahya Jammeh of Gambia. He has given public sector workers an extra day off each week saying: "this new arrangement will allow Gambians to devote more time to prayers, social activities and agriculture – going back to the land and grow what we eat and eat what we grow, for a healthy and wealthy nation".

While it's unlikely that a four day week would encourage many people in the UK to grow their own food, more time for social activities and to devote to general well-being might be welcome.

There have been previous large-scale experiments. The state of Utah in the United States tried this in 2008. Most of the 25,000 workforce were put on a four day week and most public buildings were closed on Fridays. Only essential safety services and a few other staff remained working on the fifth day.

People using official services managed to adapt to the four day week. In fact, many people liked the fact that offices were open longer each day as they could contact them in the early evening after their own work had finished.

Employees generally liked the scheme and savings were made (though they were not as large as predicted).

Incidental benefits included less crowding in the rush hour and a cut in carbon emissions. A change of governor meant that the state-wide scheme was discontinued, but some larger cities have retained the practice.

There are some obvious disadvantages – a ten hour long day plus a commute sounds like a treadmill. Social activities in the evening would be limited – with an effect on bars, pubs, cinemas, theatres etc. Could young children really remain in childcare, nurseries or after school clubs for that length of time?

Emergency workers obviously could not benefit and as a consequence of not sharing the same work patterns as their hours would begin to seem even more anti-social. And what about schools? Would a longer day and a longer weekend promote learning or impede it?

One of the difficulties with coming to a conclusion on the advantages and disadvantages is that while the financial results can be estimated and measured, the longer term consequences for well-being, health, family and social life are much less easy to assess.

There was a hint of the different social needs between genders in the YouGov poll - the 72% in favour was made up of 77% men but only 67% women.

The very aspects of modern life that make it more flexible – mobile technology and the internet, for example – also mean that the boundaries between work and leisure time are blurred. We can be dealing with work texts, emails, tweets in any location and at any time. We are available nearly 24/7 and we certainly expect shopping, information and services to be available to us. Would the four day week help with the work/life balance or hinder it?

So the question remains: many of us are still working 5/7 – probably an outdated pattern – but can we really work 4/10 in a 24/7 society?

Sources: Various

MY (VERY) EARLY RETIREMENT AT 33

ED HAWKINS DECIDED A LIFE OF LEISURE WOULD BE WASTED ON HIS OLD AGE. SO HE OPTED TO QUIT HIS JOB NOW AND SAVE THE RAT RACE FOR LATER. AND HE'S NOT THE ONLY ONE

Cast your eyes over your workplace. You might see 100 or so people. Statistically five of your busying or bone-idle brethren will be dead before they reach retirement age.

Could be you. Could be me, I thought. So at the age of 33, I decided to retire. Last August, I gave up my job as a journalist, rented out my London flat and with my girlfriend – who heartily agreed with the plan – moved to the south-west of France. Hectic city life and economic blues were swapped for country walks and fireside chats.

Fear – and yes, OK, a tinge of weariness – was the catalyst. I worried that I was wasting the best years of my life blinking at a computer screen. And that when eventually I did pack up work, I would have hours to kill but only aching, weary joints to strike a feeble blow.

Even the Office for National Statistics backs up this notion. The healthy life-expectancy of the average UK male is 74. In these times of austerity who knows how long we may be forced to work. The solution seemed obvious, if a little risky: retire now and work later. Youth is wasted on the young, they say... but surely retirement is wasted on the old?

Many will think us foolhardy, as did some of our friends and family, not to mention bosses. But I've discovered we're not the only ones who've chosen to live like pensioners, decades before our time. Having been in France for six months, we've met other couples who want to enjoy life in their prime and received news of friends back home who've likewise ditched high-powered careers.

These are not work-shy layabouts or trustafarians, either. They are ambitious professionals in their mid-30s or early 40s. As for me, I have worked hard. I started as a journalist at 17 and had not stopped since. Early shifts, night shifts, weekends, Bank Holidays and Christmases: check. And what was it all for? I got halfway up the ladder and realised I'm afraid of heights – or

SOME ISSUES:

Do you agree with the writer, that you spend your best years working?

What are the benefits of doing what this writer is doing... and the negatives?

What would you like to do with your life?

See also:
Complete Issues
Work

I WORRIED THAT I WAS WASTING THE BEST YEARS OF MY LIFE BLINKING AT A COMPUTER SCREEN..

...AND THAT WHEN EVENTUALLY I DID PACK UP WORK, I WOULD HAVE HOURS TO KILL BUT ONLY ACHING, WEARY JOINTS

to be precise, professional responsibility and the attendant drudgery. It should not matter that I feel this way. I am not married, I don't have kids and am damn lucky to be solvent. This is the time to relish temporary freedom.

Any doubts, fortunately, were allayed when it transpired that with careful budgeting and income from my flat, a simple, stress-free life in France was a realistic possibility. Simple being the operative word. With a tight budget, the customary trappings of London life would

have to be forgotten. We found a cosy gîte near Toulouse and travelled down in our beaten-up VW camper, an obstinate vehicle that occasionally required a push start.

So here we are, having spent the winter wining, walking and reading books by the wood burner. Stress has been reduced to wondering whether the fire will condescend to spit and crackle into life. The summer promises the chance to perfect my petanque game with the locals, to lounge by the pool and taking supper on sun-baked terraces. Our friends joke

Photo Ed Hawkins © The Independenta

WORKING IN THE CITY WAS FULL-ON. I SPENT THE LAST FIVE YEARS ALWAYS ON CALL. I TRAVELLED A LOT AND SAW MORE OF HEATHROW THAN HOME. I WAS ON MY BLACKBERRY AT SIX IN THE MORNING AND IT WAS THE LAST THING I CHECKED AT NIGHT.

SO I'VE RETIRED. NOW WE GROW OUR OWN VEGETABLES, GO SKIING IN THE PYRENEES IN THE WINTER OR SWIM EVERY DAY IN THE SUMMER

that we are a "bit young to be living like pensioners", but we counter that by telling them the daily grind seems a generation away.

Certainly those who have also opted out share that view. Yvonne and Iain Morton live in the next village and gave up their jobs as IT consultants in the City for la vie Francaise. They began a Grand Designs-style building project in 2003, converting disused tractor sheds into a home. In 2009, when Yvonne, 43, took redundancy, they moved here full-time. Iain stopped work 18 months ago when he was 43.

"Working in the City was full-on," Yvonne says. "I spent the last five years always on call. I travelled a lot and saw more of Heathrow than home. I was on my BlackBerry at six in the morning and it was the last thing I checked at night. Enough was enough. So I've retired. Now we grow our own vegetables, go skiing in the Pyrenees in the winter or swim every day in the summer.

"It's relatively cheap to live here. Baguettes, wines and cheese don't cost that much. We have an income from rental flats in London so we don't need to work. Iain takes on contract work now and then to keep his hand in or if it's an opportunity to work with people he really likes. And I know I can always do the same."

The ability to return to work was a safety net which allowed another friend, Leonora Landau, 33, to leave her job as a lawyer for "retirement" in Argentina. "I knew I could always return," she says. "And I don't believe these days that people have to stay in the same line of work for 30 years.

"This isn't something older generations understand, though. When I told my dad, he said: "Don't be so ridiculous". I think he just couldn't understand why I wanted to do it at this time of my life when I should be settling down. He's worked in the same office for his entire career and couldn't understand the concept of this break."

Instead of returning to a "cold" London flat on a Monday night, Leonora was able to enjoy the "outdoor" culture of Buenos Aires. "You pack more into the days," she says. "You eat late, have a drink outside at a bar or go to a tango club. It beats a grey, wet London."

There are risks, of course. I am not as fortunate as Yvonne and Iain, who can take on a contract whenever they fancy. Work is certainly not guaranteed when I decide to return to London.

There is also a question mark about successful repatriation. If a job is found, how to overcome the daily grind of self-doubt, to tolerate the early-morning starts and office politics once more?

Still, it will surely be worth it for the sweltering Monday afternoons when I can sit by the pool with a vin rouge in hand, listening to the rustle of hazy vineyards. Normally at that time I would be slumped at a desk, listening to the hack and whirl of the coffee machine. Now honestly, which would you prefer?

© The Independent, 22 April 2013
www.independent.co.uk

THE MILLIONAIRE STREET SWEEPER

SOME ISSUES:

Would you give up work if you became rich?

Do you agree that work is always better than being idle?

How important is the example set by a parent?

See also:
Complete Issues
Work

What would you do if you had a million dollars? Are you already imagining the grand mansion, the swimming pool, the designer clothes, the parties, the endless holidays?

Imagine instead getting up early six days a week, putting on your bright orange jacket and setting to work sweeping the streets for a salary of $200 a month.

This is exactly what 53 year old Yu Youzhen does despite having a fortune of $1.6million.

Her riches came to her after her family land was bought by the Chinese government. She used that money to buy property and she now owns 17 apartments. But the habits of her earlier life when she had worked as a farmer, cook, truck driver and then street sweeper never left her. In the 14 years she has held her current job she has never been late for work and has only asked for three days off, all to attend funerals.

Of course, it's not about the money:

"Work is not just about the salary, it makes one focused. Laziness gives rise to all sorts of bad habits," she said.

She also wants to be a role model for her children.

"I do not want to sit around idly and eat up my fortune... My son once stayed at home for two months, and I kept scolding him during that time. Now he is doing pretty well. He said to me later I was right. I was worried he would hang out with bad people and ruin our family."

So, despite her riches, Yu Youzhen is continuing to do the job she knows, doing it well and taking satisfaction in her work and the example she is setting. How many people would do the same?

Sources: Various

Debate: Is it wrong for employers to discriminate against obese people?

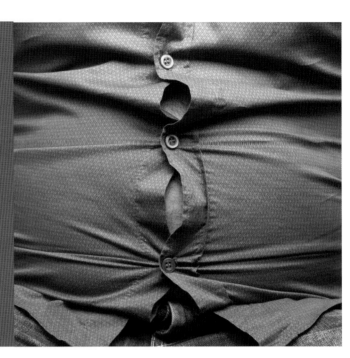

> "Some people have emotional issues to do with food. A fast-food generation need support."
> DR BUCKMAN, GP IN NORTH LONDON

> "Do they look dynamic? Do they look disciplined? Do they look highly efficient? Well, no, speaking frankly."
> KATIE HOPKINS

SOME ISSUES:

Do you agree that overweight people need support?

Do you think employers should judge people depending on their weight?

What things should employers judge people on?

If you owned a company would you choose experience over appearance?

WHAT'S GOING ON?

Single mother Jay Cole believes new laws should be brought in to stop employers discriminating against overweight people.

Appearing on This Morning yesterday, she said employers judge her 22-stone weight immediately in interviews, and dismiss her for the role, despite being keen to get off benefits and into employment.

Citing an example last week where a woman she knew got the job over her – despite failing the maths test she had passed – she claims this is discrimination similar to racism or disablism.

Apprentice star Katie Hopkins argued that she wouldn't employ anyone who was obese, and if someone suspected they were being judged negatively for their size, it is their responsibility to act and lose weight.

Figures recently published by the Department of Work and Pensions showed that more than 7,000 Britons are too fat to work. Last year, this cost the taxpayer more than £28 million in benefit payments.

CASE FOR: CHEMISTRY

It's simply naïve to think of obesity as a product of doughnut-gobbling greediness. An individual's propensity to put on fat is largely determined by genes, and losing weight is made far harder for an obese person as the chemistry in their body changes dramatically. The brain, for example, seems to stop responding to Leptin, the hormone that signals fullness. And since obesity is overwhelmingly a product of man's biology being ill-suited to modern lifestyles, what right do employers have to punish those who are obese? None. At least, no more than they can punish someone addicted to smoking.

CASE AGAINST: IMAGE

Whether we like it or not employers will take appearance into consideration when judging someone for a role. In some positions, being overweight would hinder productivity, and it is also more likely that the employee would suffer bad health and need to take time off. Presenting a positive corporate image is vital to success, and obesity can represent a lack of self-control. It is not the same as racism or disablism, and in cases where a health problem is not present, obesity can be acted on.

© The Independent, 23 February 2013
www.independent.co.uk

Young
people

Photo posed by model

The graduate breaking point

When I graduated in June I told myself I could have until the rest of the year to figure out my life and keep applying for jobs while working in a part-time position for a non-profit organisation.

Seven months later I am ready to crack and, from asking around, it seems we all are.

RACHEL HANRETTY

SOME ISSUES:

Do you have ambitions you want to achieve by a certain age?

Do you think there is pressure from society, family and friends, to achieve certain things?

Is it important to try to fulfil these goals or do they add unnecessary pressure?

When did Britain's young people become overly obsessed with reaching a landmark by a certain age? Some of us already feel guilty that in our made-up world of social obstacles we are behind.

A good chunk of my friends and fellow graduates are working unpaid because we have been told that working unpaid in the media and creative industries we so desperately want to be a part of is the key to a job. But not earning a salary? Well, that's being behind in the game.

I admire these friends though, at least they are committed to doing what they want to do. I have seen some already peel away to work in well paid jobs but sacrifice their soul to do so. Cleverly though, their boring jobs help them climb over the obstacles.

Earn a certain salary, meet the person you're going to marry, get engaged (age 26 preferably), be promoted, have an amazing wedding in a venue no one else in your gaggle of friends have found (age 27), buy the house of your dreams (29), have children (30), have more children, put money aside for a nest egg, go on package holidays, do DIY on the next perfect house, entertain

Earn a salary,
get engaged,
be promoted,
have an amazing
wedding (27),
buy the house
of your dreams
(29), have
children (30),
go on package
holidays, do
DIY, do work
for charity,
retire, the big
sleep.

And that's it.

neighbours and friends with a spread of cocktail sausages and hummus dips, do work for charity, look after your ageing parents, set up your own funeral plan at the Co-op, put your children through university, retire, the big sleep.

And that's it.

Over 15 years after those Trainspotting posters started appearing on everyone's walls, we are still following its instructions: Choose Life. Choose a job. Choose a career. Choose a family.

It sounds awful. I come close to having panic attacks when I look around and realise that's what lies ahead of me. For goodness sake, I only have six and a half childless years left according to the life plan!

Yet we secretly want to know that that's the safe trajectory we will all take. It's safe and cosy even if I know

I'll end up looking behind me and thinking of what could have been.

So I'm stuck between wanting to be put in a box with a label and running far, far away from predictability to do something I want to do which I can live off and cope with knowing that my life will never reach the obstacles on society's life map.

I'm clinging on to the shreds of blissful naivety that carried me through to the end of 2012. I don't want to grow up and become conventional, in a box with a label. But will I ever set up the businesses I dream of, publish the novel that hides in a drawer, or write that film script?

Who knows? I guess I have to prepare for being uncomfortable first and live with that.

To everyone who is going through the same thing, know that you're not the only

one who is losing their mind. To those who might be living with a recent graduate who is coming close to having this sort of breakdown, please be patient. And if you are a parent who has followed the life path to a tee, don't say anything at all.

Herald Scotland, 21 January 2013

You can read more of Rachel's blogs here: www.rachelhanretty.co.uk

Photo posed by model

It isn't easy being young in the United Kingdom today

One in five of NEETs (16 to 25 year olds not in employment, education or training) said they 'cannot cope with everyday life' – CAROLINE MORTIMER

SOME ISSUES:

Do you think there is a difference between the issues your parents faced as young people compared to your generation?

Do news reports about youth unemployment deter you from pursuing a career?

Does the writer have a good case or is she 'simply whining'?

Selected from Complete Issues:
Effects of unemployment
Fact File 2013 p190
Actually, the kids are alright
Essential Articles 14 p206

Martina Milburn, chief executive of the Prince's Trust, calls us 'the lost generation'.

Lost because more and more of us are facing long term unemployment, mounting debt and declining hope of change.

The 'lost' generation, the 'jilted' generation, the 'forgotten' generation; whatever way you want to put it, it isn't easy being young in the United Kingdom today.

So it's no wonder a report released by the Prince's Trust last week shows that one in ten of us feel we 'cannot cope with everyday life', this number rising to one in five of NEETs, 16 to 25 year olds not in employment, education or training.

The survey of 2,136 young people by the charity showed half of respondents admitted to feeling depressed "always" or "often".

A further 22 per cent also said they felt they had no one to talk to.

This is not surprising given it feels like no-one is listening.

No matter how many times I, or one of my contemporaries, attempt to make the case for youth disillusionment there are many for whom it falls on deaf ears.

We are 'lazy', we are 'spoilt', we expect too much without too much work. We're feckless, we're even 'feral' and 'in the good old days' we knew our place.

Many believe young people are simply whining because we've been spoilt by the prosperity of the past 20 years. That because they earned little money and worked hard for it when they were young, my generation should shut up and do the same.

But what they fail to realise is they entered the workforce during an era of either full employment or

We were promised the earth, we were told we could do anything and everything with a university degree. Now this has been exposed as a lie.

a time where there was a chance of paid employment further down the line.

My generation has come of age in an era where our dire employment opportunities are used as material for light entertainment and minimum wage work is seen as a privilege rather than a right.

In some senses, these people are right. We were promised the earth, we were told we could do anything and everything with a university degree. Now this has been exposed as a lie.

But that's hardly our fault is it? We didn't ask to get into mountains of debt for jobs that didn't exist. Instead of treating our crushed hopes and dreams with contempt, maybe it's time for a little compassion?

We are constantly told to grow up but are repeatedly infantilised by society. We aren't listened to by politicians but expected to follow the rules they set for us. We are forced to depend on our mothers and fathers because we can't find a paying job yet are supposed to 'work hard'.

We have all the responsibilities of regular members of society but none of the same rights.

Societal participation is supposed to be a two way street. We have been denied everything we were promised and society is making little attempt to help us. Yet we are still expected to do as we're told, keep our heads down and be grateful for any scrap of charity thrown our way.

Why should we do what we're told when we get nothing in return? People say we're ungrateful but what do we have to be grateful for? Long term unemployment? Debt? Unpaid work?

The question is: why should we? Why should we do what we're told when we get nothing in return? People say we're ungrateful but what do we have to be grateful for? Long term unemployment? Debt? Unpaid work?

Why shouldn't we shout and scream? Why shouldn't we march on a government that thinks young people should accept less and do more?

It's a miracle that we don't. In fact this report shows not a sense of anger amongst young people but a sense of bewilderment and fear. We are the lost generation. Lost because we don't know what to do now, scared of what the future brings but having no idea how to escape from the trap society laid for us.

Simply put, my generation is scared of being left behind. Despite the potential

Simply put, my generation is scared of being left behind.

improvement to the economy, young people risk becoming 'unemployable' because they could get stuck in the NEET wasteland for too long.

Forgotten and ignored, we don't necessarily want sympathy, we just need help. This is not necessarily it for us. There are so many bright, talented people in this country who can certainly 'strive' for and achieve more. Yet we can't do it alone. We need guidance, support and, most importantly, compassion from our elders.

Society has already failed us once, if we're left to get on with it alone now society will have failed us for a second time.

All young people want is dignified, paid and secure employment. I fail to see why that makes us 'spoilt'.

© The Independent, 8 January 2013
www.independent.co.uk

Something in the way children are now brought up and educated seems to stop them from wanting to grow up – or even having the freedom to

SUSAN ELKIN

WHY DON'T WE ENCOURAGE YOUNG PEOPLE TO GROW UP?

SOME ISSUES:

Do you agree there is a difference between young people today and their parents' generation?

Are modern parents too protective or just more supportive than previous generations?

What role does education play in this?

Are there other factors in society which contribute to the situation?

See also:
Grown up at 12? p206

Selected from Complete Issues:
I am an actual human being
*Essential Articles 14 p20
(see also Fact File 2014 for
statistics on childhood freedom)*

Conservative MP Claire Perry, who has three children, has just annoyed a lot of people by asserting that children are being 'babied' by over zealous parents who don't allow them to grow up independently.

That word 'babied' caught my eye because I am constantly struck by the lack of maturity in many of the young people I meet. There seems to be no will to grow up any more. Time was when there were rites of passage – first long trousers, lipstick, job, university etc and everyone desperately wanted to reach them. And for the record, at 24, I had professional training, a job and marriage under my belt, a home of my own and a baby to look after.

First stockings and nail varnish are a thing of the past. Today children usually wear miniature (often sexualised – also part of Claire Perry's

remit) versions of adult clothes just as their forebears did in the eighteenth century – along with make up and all the rest of it from babyhood in many cases.

But at the same time they are paradoxically locked in the hedonism of childhood. Something in the way 21st century children and young people are brought up and educated seems to stop them from wanting – or even having the freedom – to grow up. A sixteen year-old girl I taught in Kent, for example, told me that she had never walked out of her home alone and didn't want to. She had always been escorted by family or called for by friends. An eighteen year old apprentice at my hairdresser's told me she had to travel to the next town by

Parents are under pressure to drive or escort their children to and from school. We then expect them to stay in education for a very long time without much sense of where it's all leading.

train for classes at the FE college and was terrified because she had never travelled alone on a train.

I doubt that these are all that typical – or at least I hope not - but social commentator Frank Furedi, Emeritus Professor at the University of Kent, said last week that universities now often have to 'act like teachers by helping students along' because they arrive 'lacking a sense of maturity.'

Well perhaps the universities might look to the image they present to young people with their prospectuses and websites which glamorise student bars, social life and night life, in some cases, as if that were the main reason for enrolling. Anyone who lives in a university town will tell you that student behaviour,

especially when alcohol is involved, is a problem. And one of the bar staff in a Cambridge college told me recently that the more privileged, protected and over parented the background of student the more likely he or she, once off the leash, is to be unable to cope with student life in a mature and sensible way.

It confirms what I hear everywhere I go. I recently interviewed Paul Roseby, artistic director of the wonderful and highly respected National Youth Theatre. He told me that NYT has just extended its age range upwards to 25. 'Well they stay young for longer these days don't they?' he replied when I asked him why and of course he's right.

Claire Perry's point was that mothers, especially if they've come out of high flying jobs to

care for their children, are inclined to micro manage their children like business projects. Instead of allowing them space and time to dream, drift, play and think. Parents often organise every available minute into arranged activity. And that, she says, means that children become over dependent on their parents.

I think the problem goes much further than that. There is something about the whole of present day education – which in many cases now lasts for at least 18 years from age three to 21 – which infantilises children and young people. We lock them into schools (most primary schools are now reminiscent of prisons) for fear of paedophiles – and litigation if anything goes wrong. Parents are under pressure to drive or escort their children to and from school for the same reasons. We then expect them to stay in education for a very long time – largely because it keeps the unemployment figures down – without much sense of where it's all leading.

The school curriculum – in which everything is painstakingly specified – has a lot to answer for too. Part of growing up is learning to think independently even when your point of view is different from everyone else's. 'If you can keep your head when all about you are losing theirs' as Kipling put it.' Fat chance in most lessons these days. An awful lot of teaching is now very formulaic and dominated by aims, objectives, learning outcomes and other bits of jargon which seem to get in the way of developmental learning. Result? Herd mentality.

And they are for the most part a herd of lambs rather than sheep. Ovine Peter Pans.

© *The Independent, 4 March 2013*
www.independent.co.uk

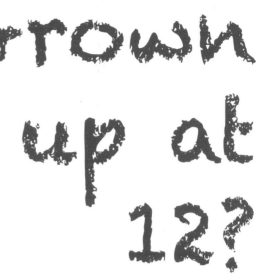

Grown up at 12?

For their own generation, childhood ended at 16 but parents who completed a survey for Netmums think their own children have lost out on precious years of childhood. Over 70% of parents polled said their child was no longer childlike by the age of 12.

> *Children need time to grow and emotionally mature in order to cope with what life throws at them.*
>
> **Siobhan Freegard, Netmums co-founder**

Almost 90% of parents believe that modern children are under much greater pressure and grow up far faster than previous generations.

For boys, the pressures were to be 'macho' before they were ready and to be good at everything, schoolwork, sports, relationships.

SOME ISSUES:

Do you agree that young people are no longer children by the time they reach 12?

Are the parents right to be worried about the 'pressures' on their children?

Are modern children being asked to cope with more pressures earlier than they are ready?

See also:
Why don't we encourage young people to grow up? p204

Selected from Complete Issues:
Don't primp children out of their innocence
Essential Articles 15 p97

For girls, the main worry was their appearance. 45% of parents said their daughter felt pressure to 'be thin'. Over half said their girls worried about being liked and how many 'friends' they had on Facebook. More than a quarter felt their daughter was being pushed into an interest in sex and boyfriends before she was mature enough to cope.

75% of parents felt the main push to grow up too quickly came from friends and schoolmates. But large numbers also mentioned the internet, celebrity culture and magazines for youngsters which had content more suited to older age groups.

They were angry, too, at inappropriately sexy clothes being sold.

Parents were devastated by the comparison between current childhood and their memories of their own. 83% of them said they were still childlike at age 12 and their favourite activity was playing outdoors with friends. For modern teens the top choice was playing alone on an iPad or tablet.

Source: Netmums

Complete
Issues

understanding our world

Section names are in capitals and in colour.

Page numbers refer you to the article rather than the specific term.

When you use this index for research it refers to articles within this book. When you enter a search term online using Complete Issues, you can search this volume and previous ones as well as Fact File for related statistics and Key Organisations for relevant contacts.

www.completeissues.co.uk

Index

Published by Carel Press Ltd
4 Hewson St, Carlisle CA2 5AU
Tel +44 (0)1228 538928,
Fax 591816
office@carelpress.co.uk
www.carelpress.co.uk
This collection © 2014
Christine A Shepherd & Chas White

COPYRIGHT NOTICE
Reproduction from this resource is allowed for use within the purchasing school, college or library only. Copyright is strictly reserved for all other purposes and remains with the original copyright holder.

Acknowledgements
Designer: Anne Louise Kershaw
Editorial team: Anne Louise Kershaw, Debbie Maxwell, Christine A Shepherd, Chas White
Subscriptions: Ann Batey (Manager), Brenda Hughes, Anne Maclagan

We wish to thank all those writers, editors, photographers, press agencies and wire services who have given permission to reproduce copyright material. Every effort has been made to trace copyright holders of material but in a few cases this has not been possible. The publishers would be glad to hear from anyone who has not been consulted.

Cover design:
Jack Gregory and Anne Louise Kershaw
Front cover photos: Clockwise from top left – police image © veroxdale/Shutterstock.com, Mick & Mairead Philpott © Rui Vieira/PA Archive/Press Association Images, Jessica Ennis © David Davies/PA Archive/Press Association Images, Prince © Northfoto/Shutterstock.com, Displaced persons © UNHCR/H. Gaux, November 2012, young orangutan © The Orangutan Foundation, Displaced woman © UNHCR/G. Gordon, January 2013

British Library Cataloguing in Publication Data

Essential Articles 2014: The articles you need on the issues that matter
1. Social problems – Study and teaching (Secondary) – Great Britain 2. Social sciences – Study and teaching (Secondary) – Great Britain
I. Shepherd, Christine A
II. White, C
361.00712 41
ISBN 978-1-905600-40-3

Printed by Finemark, Poland